Soothing the Heart of the Bereaved

At the time of the loss of children and loved ones

Musakkin al-Fuād

'inda Faqd al-Ahibba wal Awlād.

Second Martyr
Sheikh Zayn ad-Din Ali ibn Muhammad al-Jab'i al-Amili

Translated by
Yasin T. al-Jibouri

Copyright © 2021 by Yasin T. al-Jibouri

All rights reserved. No part of this publication may be reproduced, distributed, or transmitted in any form or by any means, including photocopying, recording, or other electronic or mechanical methods, without the prior written permission of the publisher, except in the case of brief quotations embodied in critical reviews and certain other noncommercial uses permitted by copyright law. For permission requests, write to the publisher, addressed "Attention: - Permissions (*Soothing the Heart of the Bereaved*)," at the email address below.

       Lantern Publications
       info@lanternpublications.com
       www.lanternpublications.com

Ordering Information:
Quantity sales. Special discounts are available on quantity purchases by corporations, associations, and others. For details, contact the distributor at the address below.

       Shia Books Australia
       www.shiabooks.com.au
       info@shiabooks.com.au

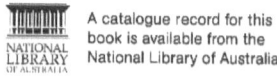 A catalogue record for this book is available from the National Library of Australia

ISBN- 978-1-922583-19-2

Second Edition
The Arabic text can be found here: Link:
http://alkafeel.net/islamiclibrary/morality/maskenfuad/index.html

In the Name of God,
the Most Compassionate, the Most Merciful

Prayers of God's Peace and Blessings

In keeping with the Islamic practice of showing respect for the name of God ﷻ and sending prayers of God's ﷻ peace and blessings whenever the name of His blessed Prophet, Lady Fāṭima, and the Twelve Imams is mentioned, as well as for asking God ﷻ to hasten the reappearance of the Lord of the Age on the Earthly plane, one or more of the following Arabic symbols have been employed throughout the text. They are repeated for their great rewards.

  Used exclusively after the name of God ﷻ, meaning "the Sublimely Exalted", or, as a prayer, "[May His name be] Sublimely Exalted".

  Used exclusively after the name of the Prophet, meaning "May the peace and blessings of God ﷻ be unto him and unto [the purified and inerrant members of] his family"

  Used for any of the Twelve Imams or past prophets of God ﷻ, meaning "May God's ﷻ peace be unto him".

  Used for two or more of the Twelve Imams or past prophets of God ﷻ, meaning "May God's ﷻ peace be unto them".

  Used for Lady Fāṭima, meaning "May God's ﷻ peace be unto her".

  Used for a plurality of the Fourteen Immaculate ones, meaning "May God's ﷻ peace be unto them all collectively".

 Used for the Lord of the Age (the Twelfth Imam), meaning "May God ﷻ hasten the advent of his noble person".

Table of Contents

Preface — 7
- *Reason behind writing this book* — 12
- *About the Author* — 16
- *Method of critique:* — 18

Introduction — 21
- *Core principles* — 23

1 - Rewards for the loss of children — 41
- *More on rewards for loss of children from other sources* — 59

2 - Patience and its aftermath — 65
- Perseverance in face of calamity and its rewards — 73
- Perseverance upon the calamity of death — 78
- Perseverance during forms of affliction — 84
- *Denunciation Of Ancient Customs On Death Of Sons And Loved Ones* — 88
- *Some women's perseverance as reported by scholars* — 100

3 - Acceptance — 119
- *Acceptance- A Golden path* — 129
  - The First Degree of Acceptance — 130
  - The Second Degree of Acceptance — 131
  - The Third Degree of Acceptance — 132
- *Reference To A Group Of Ancestors Whose Acceptance Of Destiny As Transmitted By Scholars* — 135

4 - Weeping — 141
- *Significance of saying "Inna Lillahi wa Inna Ilayhi Raji'oon* — 154

5 – On Mourning — 157
- *How To Console* — 165
- *Mourning on the loss of loved ones* — 168
- *Mourning over calamities* — 173

6 – Conclusion — 179

The Names and Dates of the Twelve Imams

No	Kunya	Name	Dates of Birth-Death Islamic	Christian
1	Ab'al-Hasan	Ali b. AbuTalib	-23 to 40	600–661
2	Abu Md.	Hasan ibn Ali	3–50	624–670
3	Abu Abdillah	Husayn ibn Ali	4–61	626–680
4	Abu Md.	Ali ibn Husayn	38–95	658–712
5	Abu Ja'far	Md. ibn Ali	57–114	677–732
6	Abu Abdillah	Ja'far ibn Md.	83–148	702–765
7	Ab'al-Hasan	Mūsā b. Ja'far	128–183	744–799
8	Ab'al-Hasan	Ali ibn Mūsā	148–203	765–817
9	Abu Ja'far	Md. ibn Ali	195–220	810–835
10	Ab'al-Hasan	Ali ibn Md.	212–254	827–868
11	Abu Md.	Hasan ibn Ali	232–260	846–874
12	Ab'al-Qāsim	Md. Ibn Hasan	255–Present	868–Present

A Note on Transliteration

The transliteration system used in this book is basically that of the ICAS Press (2015) method (which is based on the Library of Congress Romanization Tables), with the following changes: Persian words of Arabic origin are transliterated as they are pronounced in the Arabic language, rather than their Persian pronunciations. However, Persian words, proper names, and personal names are transliterated to reflect their proper Persian pronunciation. Thus, 'Bukhāri' is Bokhāri, Kulayni is Kolayni, etc. In such cases, the sound for the *kasra* is romanized by 'e' rather than by 'i', the *ḍamma* by 'o' rather than by 'a' or 'u'. Similarly, the ض, ذ, and ظ letters are all romanized by the letter 'z' (for Persian words only). Thus, the *ezāfe* (*iḍāfa*) is Romanized -*e* after a consonant, and -*ah* or -*ye* after a vowel.

Preface

Due to lack of want, outgiving and generosity, He has willed to shower His blessings unto the descendants of Adam ﷺ with generosity, blessing them first with the bliss of existence and getting them out of the sphere of void. Then He put everything on earth at their disposal, making them the masters of this planet, faring with its soil, water, and atmosphere as they wish. He has subjected to them its animals, plants, minerals, and all other treasures. He then bestowed upon them guidance by sending them messengers and divine books which secure for them the pleasure of their Lord, their own happiness, sustenance, and goodly return if they obey Him.

After all these generous blessings and clear guidance comes testing and examining, and these cannot take place without affliction of the decrease of a blessing or an affliction in self and in wealth, and it is here when a steadfast person who seeks rewards is distinguished from one who is impatient, fretful.

The most Praised One has promised to give them generous rewards, to pay them their dues without count, informing them that He, the most Exalted One, supports them if they persevere.

Imam al-Bāqir has said, "A believer is tested in the life of this world according to the extent of his faith" or he said "according to the extent of his belief"[1]. Imam al-Sādiq has said, "If Allah loves one of His servants, He exposes him to trials, one after the other."[2] He also said, "Great rewards accompany great trials."[3] This is why among people, according to traditions, there are those who are tested more severely such as the prophets, then the *walī* or guardians, then the most pious, and so on.[4]

The Prophet said, "We, prophets, are tried the most, and we are followed in this regard by the believers, the most pious then the less pious, and so on. One who tastes the sweet taste of trial, under a protective covering from Allah, finds it tastier than a bliss."[5]

He has equaled obedience to Allah through patience to half of one's *iman* (conviction), regarding it as one of the keys to achieving rewards and determining patience as occupying a position in *iman* equal to that of the head to the body; there is no body without a head; therefore, one without patience is without *iman*, and one who is patient will receive rewards equal to those due to one thousand martyrs.

---

[1] *Al-Kāfi*, Vol. 2, p. 197; *Mishkat Al-Anwar*, p. 298.

[2] *Ibid.*, Vol. 2, pp 6, 197.

[3] *Ibid.*, Vol. 2, p. 3

[4] This is narrated by al-Kolayni in his book *Al-Kāfi*, Vol. 2, pp. 11, 196, by Ibn Majah in his *Sunan*, Vol. 2, pp. 1334, 4023, by al-Tirmidhi in his *Sunan*, Vol. 4, pp. 28, 2509, by Ahmed in his *Musnad*, Vol. 1, pp. 172, 180, 185, by al-Darmi in his *Sunan*, Vol. 2, p. 320 and by al-Hakim al-Naishapuri in his *Mustadrak*, Vol. 1, p. 41 with some minor variation in wording.

[5] *Musbah al-Shari'a*, p. 487.

It is for the above reason that Imam Ali ﷺ has said, "If you are patient, destiny will be affected in your regard and you will receive your rewards, but if you fret, destiny will be affected in your regard as you bear the burden of your sins."[6] Imam al-Kadim ﷺ, has said, "If one beats on his thigh when afflicted by a calamity, he voids his rewards."[7]

Calamities differ one from another. They range from a chronic illness to a demeaning condition, to the loss of wealth..., etc. One of the most difficult however, is the loss of loved ones and especially of children. Many narrations have been transmitted in this regard, for instance, the Holy Prophet ﷺ is reported to have said "If one loses three of his sons while maintaining his patience, he will be sheltered from the fire by permission of Allah ﷻ, and this will be a sure protection for him."[8]

Allah ﷻ asked Dawood (David) ﷺ, "What is the equivalent of this son for you?" Dawood ﷺ answered, "He was worth the fill of the earth with gold." Allah ﷻ said, "Then you will have on the Day of Judgment the fill of the earth rewards."[9]

The greatest Prophet ﷺ went further than that when he said, "... I shall brag about you to other nations till a stillborn stay at the gate of Paradise

---

[6] *Nahjul-Balagha*, Vol. 3, pp. 224, 291. [This is referring to the 3 Vol English translation as translated by Yasin T. Al-Jibouri published by Authorhouse (2013)]

[7] *Al-Kāfi*, Vol. 3, pp. 9, 225.

[8] *Al-Jami` Al-Kabīr*, Vol. 1, p. 817.

[9] Sheikh Waram has narrated it in his book titled *Tanbih Al-Khawatir*, Vol. 1, p. 287 and by al-Suyuti in his book *Al-Durr Al-Manthūr*, Vol. 5, p. 306 with some variations in its wording.

refusing to enter, and it will be told to enter, but it will say, 'I and my parents?!' The response will be, 'You and your parents'."¹⁰

Many traditions have been transmitted about offering condolences to one who is afflicted by a calamity to lighten it for him. Ibn Mas`ūd quotes the Prophet ﷺ as saying, "One who offers condolences to a person who is afflicted by a calamity will receive as many rewards as those received by the afflicted person."¹¹ Similarly, Abu Barzah is quoted as saying that the Messenger of Allah ﷺ has said, "If one offers condolences to a mother who lost her child, he will be outfitted with coats in Paradise."¹²

Weeping over someone who has died does not decrease rewards, nor does it diminish one's rewards. The first person who wept over a son whom he lost was our father Adam ﷺ who mourned Able ﷺ and composed famous verses of poetry recorded in books, grieving over him a great deal. The condition of Jacob (Ya`qub) ﷺ is more famous than needs mentioning, so much so that he wept so much till he lost his eyesight over Joseph (Yusuf) ﷺ.

As regarding our master, Ali son of al-Husayn ﷺ, he wept over his father for forty years, fasting during the day and spending the night standing for prayers. Whenever it was time for him to break his fast, his servant would bring him his food and drink, putting them in front of him: "Eat, master!" The Imam ﷺ would say, "The son of the Messenger

---

¹⁰ This has been narrated by al-Suyuti in his book *Al-Jami` Al-Saghir*, Vol. 2, pp. 55, 4724 and by al-Muttaqi al-Hindi in *Muntakhab Kanz Al-Ummal*, Vol. 6, p. 390, both quoting Ibn Abbas.

¹¹ *Al-Jami` Al-Kabir*, Vol. 1, p. 801.

¹² Al-Tirmidhi, *Sunan*, Vol. 2, pp. 269, 1082.

of Allah ﷺ was killed as he was hungry; the son of the Messenger of Allah ﷺ was thirsty...," and he would keep repeating these statements and weeping till his tears would wet his food. He kept doing so for the entirety of his life.[13] The Messenger of Allah ﷺ for this [same] reason said [when his son Ibrahim died], "The eyes are tearful, the heart is grieved, and we will not say anything that incurs the wrath of the Lord."[14]

Among those who did very well maintaining their patience on the loss of loved ones and sons was Abu Dharr al-Ghifari, may Allah be pleased with him, none of whose sons lived long. He used to say, "Praise be to Allah ﷻ who takes them away from the transient abode to lodge them into the abode of eternity."[15] These men provide us with the best and greatest moral lessons, and they are our role models; many are those who are patient and who anticipate rewards in the cause of Allah ﷻ.

Among those who were hit by this affliction and lost loved ones and children is our mentor, the Second Martyr, may Allah sanctify his pure soul. The author of *Rawdāt Al-Jannāt*[16] has recorded his calamity and loss of children who died young. Sayyid al-Amin says, "His children did not last long but many of the males passed away before Sheikh Hasan about whose survival he was not sure either."[17]

---

[13] *Al-Luhoof fi Qatla Al-Tufoof*, p. 87.

[14] Ibn Majah, *Sunan*, Vol. 1, pp. 506, 1589 and *Muntakhab Kanz Al-Ummal*, Vol. 6, p. 265.

[15] This tradition has been narrated by al-Muttaqi al-Hindi in his book *Muntakhab Kanz Al-Ummal*, Vol. 1, p. 212 and is cited by al-Majlisi in his work *Bihar Al-Anwar*, Vol. 82, p. 142.

[16] *Rawdāt Al-Jannāt*, Vol. 3, p. 379.

[17] *A`yān Al-Shi`a*, Vol. 7, p. 144.

Talking about Sheikh Hasan, the son of the second Martyr, Sheikh Abbas al-Qummi says, "He was not expected to live because of the calamities which had afflicted his father. Many of his siblings, who were born before him [Sheikh Hasan], had died [young]."[18]

Reason behind writing this book

The writing of *Musakkin al-Fuād* was not the product of a purely scholarly condition dictated by the reality of class and teaching or due to the need of debates at the *hawza* as much as it was the outcome of a conscientious and emotional condition lived by the Second Martyr with all his senses and faculties with which he interacted positively throughout his honorable life. Most references which narrate the biography of the Second Martyr indicate that he was tried by the death of his sons when they were still quite young, so much so that he had no hope that any of them would stay alive. None of them was spared death save his son Sheikh Hasan about whose survival he was not sure at all. He was martyred when his son was four or seven years old.

The Second Martyr, may he be sanctified, confronted the condition of family deprivation with the loftiest degrees of patience and perseverance, so he wrote *Musakkin al-Fuād* (Soother of the heart [that is burning deep with passion and emotion]) while his heart was dripping with pain and sighs as he watched his sons die as fresh flowers snapped away before his very eyes. In the introduction to his afore-mentioned book, he, may Allah be pleased with him, says, "Since death is the great event, the cause of a permanent separation from loved ones, and since the separation of a loved one is considered to be among the

---

[18] *Al-Kuna wal Alqāb*, Vol. 2, p. 349.

greatest calamities, so much so that the heart of any wise person almost changes its place, the heart of anyone known for having a sound mind, especially since the most loved ones are the sons who bring happiness to one's heart..., for this reason, such separation deserves great rewards, and the parents are promised intercession on the Day of Judgment on account of their loss. For this reason, I have gathered in this dissertation some Prophetic legacies, the conditions of those who achieved supreme perfections, in addition to brief yet clear hints so, by the will of Allah the Almighty, rust may be removed from the hearts of the deprived and grief may be removed from those grieved. Rather, on its account the hearts of those who have knowledge are elated, those who regard it as a tradition of the unaware may wake up from their slumber. I have called it *The Soother of the Heart at the Time of the Loss of Loved Ones and of Children*, organizing it in an Introduction, chapters and a conclusion."[19]

Musakkin al-Fuād, though small in size, is distinguished for its unique subject. This makes it a reliable reference and unique of its kind according to a group of authors of narrative encyclopedias such as 'Allama al-Majlisi in his *Bihār al-Anwār*, Sheikh al-Hurr in *Al-Jawāhir al-Saniyya*, Sheikh al-Nawari in his *Mustadrak al-Wasā'il*, and others.

'Allāma al-Majlisi says the following in his *Bihār al-Anwār* to explain his sources: "... and *Musakkin al-Fuād*... by the Second Martyr, may Allāh elevate his status."[20]

In his Introduction to *Al-Jawāhir al-Saniyya*, Sheikh al-Hurr says, "I have quoted the traditions in it from authentic and respected books as

---

[19] *Musakkin Al-Fuād*, p. 17.
[20] *Bihār Al-Anwār*, Vol. 1, p. 19.

well as edited and reliable references", and our book is one of these respected authentic books.

Sayid Khonsari, in the process of talking about the book *Musakkin al-Fuād*, says, "His book has great benefits, rare traditions and spiritual niceties the like of which are seldom found in a book."[21]

Sayyid Muhsin al-Ameen, in his biography of the second martyr, says, "He distinguished himself for writing about subjects about which others did not write or wrote but did not say enough such as patience at the loss of loved ones and sons."[22] Recounting his works, he said, "His book titled *Musakkin al-Fuad* is one the subject of which was never discussed by anyone before him."[23]

Sheikh Tahrani mentions it in his *Dharī`a* saying, "*Musakkin al-Fuad* by the happy Sheikh Zain ad-Din ibn Ahmed al-`Āmili, the martyr, is arranged in an introduction, chapters and a conclusion. The first chapter deals with heavenly rewards for losing children, the second with patience, the third with acceptance [of destiny] and the fourth with weeping."[24]

Isma`eel Pasha, in his work *Idāh al-Maknoon*, says, "*Musakkin al-Fuad* was written by Zain ad-Din bin Ali bin Ahmed al-`Āmili, the Shiite."[25] Ibn al-`Awwadi, in his book *Bughyat al-Mureed fil Kashf an Ahwāl al-Sheikh Zain ad-Din al-Shahīd*, while stating the latter's works, says, "…

---

[21] *Rawdāt Al-Jannāt*, Vol. 3, p. 379.

[22] *A`yān Al-Shī`a*, Vol. 7, p. 145.

[23] *Ibid.*, Vol. 7, p. 156.

[24] *Al-Dharī`a*, Vol. 21, pp. 20, 3747.

[25] *Idāh Al-Maknoon*, Vol. 4, p. 479.

and one of them is the book *Musakin al-Fuād inda Faqd al-Ahibba wal Awlād.*"[26]

In the work *Amal al-Āmil*, he is said as having written a list of books which includes "... the book *Musakin al-Fuād inda Faqd al-Ahibba wal Awlād.*"[27] Sheikh Yousuf al-Bahrāni says the following in his book *Lu'lu'at al-Bahrain*: "... and he, may he be sanctified, wrote a number of books one of which is *Musakin al-Fuād inda Faqd al-Ahibba wal Awlād.*"[28]

One of the indications of the interest of the biographer, may he be sanctified, in our book, this one, is that he abridged it in another book, calling it *Mubarrid al-Akbād: Mukhtasar Musakkin al-Fuad* which is mentioned by Sheikh Ali, grandson of the Second Martyr[29], by Sheikh al-Hurr al-`Āmili[30], Sheikh Yousuf al-Bahrāni[31], Sayyid Khonsari[32], Sayyid Muhsin al-Ameen[33] and Sheikh Aqa Buzurg Tehrani[34].

It is translated into Persian by Isma`eel Khan who named it *Tasliyat al-`Ibād*. In his *Dharī`a*, Sheikh Tehrani says, "It is called *Tasliyat al-`Ibād fi Tarjamat Musakkin al-Fuad* by the martyred Sheikh and is translated

---

[26] *Bughyat Al-Murīd* as quoted in the book *Al-Durr Al-Manthūr*, Vol. 2, p. 187.
[27] *Amal Al-Āmil*, Vol. 1, p. 87.
[28] *Lu'lu'at Al-Bahrain*, p. 35.
[29] *Ad-Durr Al-Manthūr*, Vol. 2, p. 189.
[30] *Amal Al-Āmil*, Vol. 1, p. 87.
[31] *Lu'lu'at Al-Bahrain*, p. 35.
[32] *Rawdāt Al-Jannāt*, Vol. 3, p. 379.
[33] *A`yān Al-Shī`a*, Vol. 7, p. 145.
[34] *Al-Dharī`a*, Vol. 20, pp. 209, 2613.

into Persian by Isma`eel Khan Dabeer al-Sultanah who is nicknamed "glory of the men of letters", the contemporary scholar who neighbors the Shrine of Imam al-Ridha and who died in 1321 A.H. (1903 A.D.) following the completion of the translation."[35]

About the Author

His name is Sheikh Noor ad-Din Ali ibn Ahmed ibn Muhammed ibn Ali ibn Jamal ad-Din ibn Taqi ibn Salih ibn Musharraf, of `Āmil, Syria, of Toos, al-Jab`i, famously known as the "Second Martyr".

He was born on the 13th of Shawwal of 911 A.H. (March 19, 1506, according to the Gregorian calendar). His father was one of the most prominent personalities of his time, and so were his forefathers up to Salih. The same applies to the sons of his uncles, his brother Abdul-Nabi, and his nephew. Knowledge serialized in his home for a long period of time, so much so that his lineage is called "the golden chain". His son, Sheikh Hasan, was also a scholarly researcher.

He, may Allah ﷻ have mercy on his soul, studied the sciences known during his time, and examined the work of the Shiite as well as Sunni scholars. He, may Allah ﷻ be merciful to him, excelled and surpassed his peers despite his extreme poverty and hardship of living conditions. He used to guard his vineyard during the night and sometimes worked in trade while taking care of the needs of his family.

He traveled to Istanbul, then the capital of the Ottoman State, and in 18 days he wrote a dissertation in solving ten problems in sciences. He, therefore, was assigned to teach at the Nawari School in Baalbek, one

---

[35] *Ibid.*, Vol. 4, pp. 179, 882.

of the greatest schools, where he stayed for five years teaching according to the five schools of Islamic thought, a great feat for him and an indication of vast knowledge which cannot be surpassed. He wrote about eight books the most famous of which is *Al-Rawda al-Bahiyya fi Sharh al-Lum'a al-Dimashqiyya*, a book regarded as a major reference for *fiqh* studies at Shiite *hawzas*.

The sectarian fanaticism, however, a disease which has afflicted the Muslims, did not leave this brilliant scholar to be of benefit for people with his knowledge and demeanor: The fire of envy burnt in the hearts of those who let the Islamic nation reach its present condition of weakness and backwardness. They schemed plots against him, instigated rulers against him till he was arrested during the pilgrimage season inside the holy precincts of Venerable Mecca. He was taken in custody to Istanbul.

The hoodlums who arrested him were concerned about his arrival at Istanbul where he would be able to prove his innocence from the charges against him, against his pure and innocent soul; so, Satan ordered them to speed up the implementation of their scheme: They killed him on the way and carried his severed head to the capital.

His martyrdom, may he be sanctified, took place in 965 A.H. (1558 A.D.) when he was 55.

One of his students, Ibn al-Awwadi, wrote his biography in an independent dissertation which he titled *Bughyat al-Mureed fil Kashf an Ahwal al Sheikh Zayn ad-Din al-Shaheed*. Looking into the following references for his biography: *Al-Durr al-Manthur*, Vol. 2, p. 149 where *Bughyat al-Mureed fil Kashf an Ahwal al Sheikh Zayn ad-Din al-Shaheed* is cited; *Amal al-Āmil*, Vol. 1, p. 85; *Riyadh al-Ulema*, Vol. 2, p. 365;

Lu'lu'at al-Bahrain, p. 28; *Naqd al-Rijal*, p. 145; *Muntaha al-Maqal*, p. 141; *Bahjat al-Āmal*, Vol. 4, p. 254; *Rawdāt al-Jannāt*, Vol. 3, p. 352; *Tanqeeh al-Maqāl*, Vol. 1, pp. 472, 4517; *Safeenat al-Bihār*, Vol. 1, p. 723; *Al-Kuna wal Alqāb*, Vol. 2, p. 344; *Hadiyyat al-Ahbāb*, p. 167; *Al-Fawā'id al-Radawiyya*, p. 186; *A`yān al-Shiī`a*, Vol. 7, p. 143; al-Zarkali's *Al-A`lām*, Vol. 3, p. 64; *Mu`jam Rijāl al-Hadīth*, Vol. 7, p. 372 and *Mu`jam al-Mu'allifeen*, Vol. 4, p. 193.

Method of critique:

We have relied in critiquing this book from three editions:

The first is the handwritten copy at the public library of Ayatollah al-Mar`ashi, the third volume included in the group numbered 444, from p. 186 to p. 249, written by Safar al-Karmani in the clear Naskh calligraphic type on a Monday, the 27th of Dhul-Qa`da of 1087 A.H., based on a copy taken from Sheikh Muhammed al-`Āmili in Syria. At the end of the book, there is a statement which concludes it by saying "Comparing this text has been done through help from Allah Almighty". Sheikh Yousuf al-Najafi, a student of the Second Martyr, has written on the last page of the said group saying that he compared the copy and completed his comparison on a Wednesday the 9th of Rabi` al-Awwal of 1088 A.H. The book contained 320 pages, the book with which we are dealing falls in 63 pages. In each page there are 16 lines size 20.5 x 10.5 cm and we have used the symbol "Sh" [for "Shaheed II"] on the book's margin.

The second is the one kept at the Tehran University Library under No. 1017. It was written in the Naskh type by Hussain ibn Muslim ibn Hussain ibn Muhammed who is famous as Ibn Sha`eer al-`Āmili, a student of the Second Martyr, in around the year 954 A.H. The copy contains the book's Introduction and some of Chapters Two, Three and Four. There is on p. 73-B a statement saying "Completed 954" in another type of handwriting. On p. 69-A, there is a statement saying "He completed its reading, may Allah ﷻ grant him success" in the handwriting of the Second Martyr. This copy is owned by Ali ibn Muhammed Husain al-Mousawi al-Shushtari on the 15th of Jumada II of the year 1268 A.H., Ali ibn Husain ibn Muhammed-Ali ibn Zayn ad-Din al-Mousawi and Ali Muhammed al-Mousawi.

The version printed on stone in Iran was written in Tehran by the son of Ali Akbar al-Gailani on a Monday, the 26th of Safar of 1310 A.H. for which we use the symbol "H ح" on the book's margin.

Based on the style followed by the Ahl al-Bayt Foundation for Revival of Legacy, the book has gone through several editing phases as follows:

1. comparison committee: Its task is to compare the handwritten copies and identify their differences,
2. *hadith* extraction committee: Its task is to extract the texts cited in the book and render them to their sources,
3. committee for verifying differences about traditionists: Its task is to confirm the results of comparing the copies regarding differences about major narrators of *hadith* and refer them to the sources that discuss *hadith* transmitters,
4. committee for correcting text: Its task is to show a verified and correct book text closer to what the author had left us. Copies have been compared so the authenticity of texts may be marked whereas others are referred to in footnotes.
5. footnotes: All the above was utilized to arrange and coordinate the footnotes.

6. final review: In it, the book in its entirety, including footnotes, is examined to detect and correct what may have been overlooked.

In conclusion, we express our sincere appreciation and regards to the honorable brothers who participated in producing this book in such a good outfit.

Ahl al-Bayt Foundation for Revival of Legacy
Qum on the 21st of Shawwal of 1407 A.H.

Introduction

All Praise is due to Allah Who has decreed the extinction and disappearance of all His servants. He affected His command on them according to His wisdom and will. He promised those who persevere regarding His destiny beautiful rewards and happiness, and He forewarned those who fret about it with plenty of His retribution and severe penalty upon their return to Him. He has pleased the hearts of the men of knowledge through His management, so this knowledge is the pleasure of their souls when submitted to His lead, this is so despite the inability of each one of them to avoid His affecting judgment even if an ignorant person goes to extremes in his stubbornness.

I testify that there is no god except Allah, the only One; there is no partner with Him, a testimony through which I avoid the horrors in the narrowness of the Gathering and its ravines. And I testify that Muhammed, Allah's peace and blessings be with him and his progeny, is His servant and messenger, the very best of those who brought glad tidings and who warned, the greatest of all those who accepted destiny and persevered about it, peace and blessing of Allah ﷺ be with him and his progeny who are the best of the best, the greatest of creation in action, the ones who suffered the most, who submitted and accepted

His decrees, peace and blessing that will reach each and every one of them individually.

Since death is the greatest of all events, the matter that forever separates the loved ones from each other. Separation from the loved ones is regarded as one of the greatest calamities, so much so that the heart of even a wise person almost fails, the heart of one known for sagacity, for being terse, particularly when we know that the greatest of those whom we love are our children who are the pleasure of the hearts. It is for this reason that generous rewards are in store for those who suffer such separation, and the parents are promised intercession on the Day of the Return in lieu of such loss.

For this reason, I have gathered in this dissertation a group of Prophetic legacies, the conditions of those who earned sublime perfections, in addition to brief yet clear admonitions which, if Allah Almighty so pleases, should remove the rust from the hearts of those aggrieved and the grief of those aggrieved is removed; rather, the hearts of the men of knowledge are even elated by it, those who regard such grief as a tradition of the indifferent ones will wake up through it, naming it "Soother of the heart upon the loss of loved ones and children", organizing it in an Introduction, Chapters and a Conclusion.

As regarding the Introduction, know that reason is the mechanism whereby Allah is known, Praise be to Him, and through it belief in the messengers and the upholding of the divine legislations are achieved. He, the Almighty, urges us to seek virtues, forewarns us of being characterized by lowly deeds, so He administers both abodes and is the causation for winning mastership of both worlds: His likeness is light in the dark, for such light must be little among some folks, so it becomes like the vision of the night-blind, and it may be more among others, so it is like daylight in the high morning time.

One who is granted reason should not disobey Him, nor should he feel comfortable about his own absent-mindedness or inclinations. Rather, he must make Him a judge for himself and against his own *nafs*. He should refer to Him for guidance: He will then reveal to him whatever is required to make one pleased by what Allah, Praise and Exaltation belong to him, decrees especially with regard to whatever calamity has afflicted him on account of such separation.

Core principles

This is achieved through many aspects to some of which we refer here below:

FIRST

If you look at the justice and wisdom of Allah ﷻ, at the perfection of His favors and mercy, at the completion of His care of His creation, for He is the One Who brought them into being from void, showering them with great blessings, helping them with His compassion, providing them with His generous aid and assistance, all of this so they may take their share of eternal happiness and perpetual honor. This is not because He needs them, nor because he depends on them to affect His decree in their regard, for He is the Absolute Independent, the truly generous One.

He has commissioned them to undertake hardships, to do what is tough, so they may derive from all this, their lot and hope, and so He may test them and distinguish from among them those who do what is best. And He does not do that except only for their own benefit, for the perfection of their interests. He has sent them messengers to bring them glad tidings and to warn, and He revealed to them the books in which He has embedded notifications to the worlds. The achievement of this goal is dealt with in detail in the chapter about justice in the science of logic.

His actions, Exalted and Sanctified is He, are all for their own good: In them is the completion of honoring them. Death is one of these actions as the divine inspiration states in many verses of the Holy Qur'ān such as these:

وَمَا كَانَ لِنَفْسٍ أَنْ تَمُوتَ إِلَّا بِإِذْنِ اللَّهِ كِتَابًا مُؤَجَّلًا

"Nor can a soul die except by God's leave, the term being fixed as though in writing" (Qur'ān, 3:145);

قُلْ لَوْ كُنْتُمْ فِي بُيُوتِكُمْ لَبَرَزَ الَّذِينَ كُتِبَ عَلَيْهِمُ الْقَتْلُ إِلَى مَضَاجِعِهِمْ

"Say: Even if you had remained in your homes, those for whom death was decreed would certainly have gone forth to the place of their death" (Qur'ān, 3:154);

أَيْنَمَا تَكُونُوا يُدْرِكْكُمُ الْمَوْتُ وَلَوْ كُنْتُمْ فِي بُرُوجٍ مُشَيَّدَةٍ

"Wherever you are, death will find you, even if you are in towers built up strong and high!" (Qur'ān, 4:78);

اللَّهُ يَتَوَفَّى الْأَنْفُسَ حِينَ مَوْتِهَا

"It is Allah Who takes the souls (of men) at death" (Qur'ān, 39:42)

and other such verses.

Introduction

Had this not been the ultimate end of interest and the final destination of benefit for the weak servant of Allah ﷻ who is unaware of what is best for him, who wanders about in his delusion and absent-mindedness, Allah Almighty would not have done it. This is so because you have already come to know that He is the most merciful of all merciful ones, the most oft-giving. If your *nafs* insinuates to you the contrary to this, you should get to know that it is the veiled *shirk*(disbelief). And if you are convinced about it but you are not comfortable with it or your fear of it does not subside, it is nothing but obvious foolishness.

The above resulted from heedlessness about His wisdom, Allah Almighty, in dealing with His creation and about the goodness of His decree with regard to His beings, so much so that a worshipper pleads and calls upon Allah Almighty to have mercy on him and to respond to his plea, whereupon Allah Almighty says the following to His angels: "How should I have mercy on him by ridding him of something through which I am bestowing mercy on him?!" So, consider, may Allah Almighty have mercy on you, about this divine statement; it should suffice you in this Chapter if Allah Almighty so wills.

SECOND

If you take a look at the living conditions of the Messengers, peace be with them, and if you believe the reports they brought about issues related to this life and to the Hereafter, to the promises they made of eternal happiness. Furthermore, if you come to know that what they had brought came from Allah, the most Great, the most High, if you moreover believe that their speech is divinely protected from error and safeguarded from mistakes and inclinations, and if you hear about the rewards promised for any type of calamity as you will see and hear..., you will then find its occurrence easy, and you will come to know that you have in it, ultimate benefit and perfect perpetual happiness, and that you have prepared for yourself safeguarded treasures. Nay! You have protection, a fortress, a shield from painful torment and immense penalty of Hereafter which no human can ever withstand, nor can anyone be strong enough to tolerate, in addition to your son being your partner in this happiness! You and he, then, are the winners; so, you should not fret and lose patience.

Take this example: If something magnanimous assails you, if a lion or a snake leaps on you, or if a fire overtakes you, and if you have with you the most precious of your sons and the dearest to your heart. Additionally, there is in your company one of the prophets whose truthfulness you do not doubt, and if he tells you that if you offer your son in your stead, you and your son will be saved, but if you do not do so, you will be annihilated, while you do not know if your son will be harmed or not..., will a rational person doubt that offering the son as a sacrifice will mean achieving the safety of the son and, in addition to that, the father, too, will be safe, that this will be the ultimate benefit and that the opposite, the father and the son being exposed to harm, is nothing but a pitiful conclusion!

Perhaps many people prefer their own safety over that of their sons, offering the latter as sacrifices even if they are sure that they will be harmed as is the case when in valleys during times of famine. All this takes place during a single hour in a fire or in peril, and after it one may be transferred to comfort and to Paradise; so, what would you think about pain which remains without an end and stays for many, many "years"? Surely a "day" with your Lord of these days is like a thousand years of our own calculation. Had one of us seen hell or about to see it, he would have wished to offer his sons, wife, brother, and the tribe that shelters him, even all people of the world, so he may be spared the penalty.

$$\text{كَلَّا ۖ إِنَّهَا لَظَىٰ ۞ نَزَّاعَةً لِّلشَّوَىٰ ۞ تَدْعُو مَنْ أَدْبَرَ وَتَوَلَّىٰ ۞ وَجَمَعَ فَأَوْعَىٰ ۞}$$

"Nay! By no means! For it would be the Fire of Hell plucking out (his being) right to the skull, inviting (all) who turn their backs and turn their faces away (from what is right) and amass (wealth) and hide it (from use)!" (Qur'ān, 70:15-18).

From this onset comes what has been narrated about the Prophet ﷺ saying the following to Othman son of Madh`ūn, may Allah be pleased with him, whose son passed away so he was very grieved about it: "O son of Madh`ūn! Paradise has eight gates, while hell has seven. Does it not please you that whenever you come at any of its gates, you will find your son standing by it pleading to your Lord to grant you his intercession till Allah Almighty accepts his intercession?"

God willing, there will be many such traditions.

THIRD

You love your son to stay with you so he may be of benefit to you in your world here or in your Hereafter, and you most likely do not desire him to stay only for his own good, for such is the human nature. His benefit to you based on his stay is unknown. Rather, most often, it is thought that such benefit does not exist, for time seems to have drawn to a close, evil and absent-mindedness have prevailed over most people. The happy ones are rare, and the praised righteous ones are few. How much one benefits you, rather at least benefits himself, is unknown. His present benefit and safety from danger, as well as benefit to you, have all become known; therefore, you must not leave the known matter for the sake of the matter which is unknown, imagined or fancied. Consider the sons of most posterity; do you see anyone who benefits his parents except rarely? Or do you see one staying awake [for night prayers] except very few? If you see one such person, you must compare him with thousands who are different from him. If you regard your son as being among the rare ones rather than the majority is nothing but stupidity and absent-mindedness, for most people are similar to others in their lifetime than they are to their parents, as the Master of the *wasi* (guardians), blessings of Allah and His peace be with him, has described.

Although the individual whose similarity you seek, one who is righteous and useful according to what is apparent, what would inform you about his inner thoughts, the corruption of his intention and the doing of disservice to himself?! If you unveil his innermost, it will likely appear that his thoughts are bent on transgressions and scandals which you do not wish for yourself nor for your sons, and you wish that if your son is like that, his death is better for him than his life.

This is so if you want your son to be unique among the people, a *wali* (saint) among the righteous; so, how would it be the case if you want him only to inherit your house, orchard, animals, or such low soon-to-vanish things?! Why do you not leave him to inherit the Higher Paradise in the company of the sons of the prophets and messengers resurrected in the company of those who are secure and glad, reared if young in the lap of Sarah the mother of prophets, according to reports cited about the Master of Messengers [36], this is counted as nothing but nonsense if you only are wise enough to see it?!

---

[36] Al-Sadūq quotes on pp. 2, 316, Vol. 3 of his book *Man la Yahdaruhu Al-Faqih* Abu Abdullah saying, "Allah, the most Praised, the most Exalted,

Introduction

Had your objective been to see him as one of the firmly rooted scholars, the God-fearing good ones, and you let him inherit your knowledge and books and other means of goodness, remember also that even if all of this happens, what Allah The Almighty has promised of the rewards for losing him is even greater than your objective, as you will come to read by the will of Allah Almighty.

One example is narrated by al-Sadūq who cites Imam al-Sādiq ﷺ saying, "A single son whom a man offers is better than seventy who survive him and who become contemporaries of al-Qa'im ﷺ ".37

Consider there is a poor man who has with him a son wearing worn-out clothes whom he housed in a desolate dilapidated shed that has many beasts, and holes for snakes, scorpions, and fierce lions, and he is in his company approaching something terribly bad. A wise sage having wealth, trains, servants, high mansions and lofty stations feels pity for this poor man and for his son, so he sends some of his servants to him to say, "My master says this to you: 'I have felt pity for you on account of the condition of this run down place', and he worries about you and your son because of the perils to which you may be exposed, so he has granted you out of his own favor this mansion where your son can reside, and a great bondmaid from among his best bondmaids will serve

---

entrusted to the care of Ibrahim and [his wife] Sarah the believers' children whom they nourish from a tree in Paradise that has udders similar to those of cows in a mansion created of a pearl. On Judgment Day, they will be outfitted, perfumed, and gifted to their parents; so, they are in Paradise like kings with their parents, and this is the interpretation of the verse that says: '*And those who believe and whose families follow them in faith, to them We shall unite their families*' (Qur'an, 52:21)."

38 *Thawāb Al-A`māl*, Vol. 4, p. 233.

him till you take care of your personal needs. After that, if you come and wish to reside, he will let you accompany him in the mansion or even in a better mansion."

The poor man would say, "All this does not please me, and my son will not part with me from his run-down shed neither because I do not believe in the generous man nor due to the absence of my desire for his home and mansion, nor because I feel that my son is secure in this dilapidated shed, but such is my nature, and I do not wish to do the opposite of what my nature dictates to me."

So, how would you, having heard the description of this man, or would not count him to be among the lowest idiots and the meanest of all stupid people?! So, do not fall into a conduct which you do not wish others to commit, for you are more interested in what is best for you than anyone else.

Be informed that the snake bites, the devouring by the beasts and other perils of this life cannot be compared with the smallest calamity of the Hereafter which is earned because of what one has done in this life. Nay! It cannot be compared with the most Truthful One, Glory to Him, turning away from one and chastising him for one moment on the Judgment Day or even for one moment of being inside the fire then getting out of it quickly. So, what would you say about a chastisement that will last for a thousand years or many times this long, or a puff of the torment of hell the pain of which lingers for a thousand years, or a sting of its snakes and scorpions the pain of which lingers for, say, forty years?! What a comparison would there be between the highest mansion in the life of this world and the lowest ranking abode in Paradise?! What comparison is it between worn-out clothes of this life and their very best, in addition to the silk and brocades of Paradise?! You can make more and more such comparisons with regard to the eternal bliss of Paradise.

If you deeply contemplate on this example, looking into it through your mental vision, you will come to know that such is the conduct of a generous person, one great in spirit. Indeed, all rational people do not accept this poor man simply surrendering his son like that; rather, it is wisdom if he praises and thanks the person who makes him such an offer, expresses the appreciation that he deserves, for such is the requirement of appreciating a bliss.

FOURTH

Grumbling and anger imply a greatly lower status than that of accepting the destiny decreed by Allah The Almighty. If one does not accept it, he would place himself in a sure peril and would miss great rewards. The Almighty denounces those who feel angry about His decree saying [in a Qudsi *hadith*], "If one does not accept My destiny and is not patient about My affliction, let him worship a god other than Me."[38]

Speaking to Moses, peace be with him, when the latter said to Him, "Lead me to something which pleases You," the Almighty said, "I am pleased with your own pleasure with My decrees."[39]

The Holy Qur'ān states the following:

رَضِيَ اللَّهُ عَنْهُمْ وَرَضُوا عَنْهُ

---

[38] *Jāmi` Al-Akhbār*, p. 133; Al-Rawandi's *Da`awāt*, pp. 169, 471; *Al-Jāmi` Al-Saghīr*, Vol. 2, pp. 235, 6010.

[39] This is narrated by Al-Rawandi in his *Da`awāt*, pp. 164, 453 with minor wording variation.

"Allah is well-pleased with them, and they with Allah" (Qur'ān, 9:100).

Allah inspired to David (Dawūd) ﷺ the following: "O David! You want something while I want something (else); whatever will be shall be what I want; so, if you surrender to what I want, I shall spare you the ill of what you want, but if you do not surrender to what I want, I shall wear you out regarding what you want, and in the end, what will be shall be only what I want."[40]

Allah Almighty has said,

$$\text{لِكَيْلَا تَأْسَوْا عَلَىٰ مَا فَاتَكُمْ وَلَا تَفْرَحُوا بِمَا آتَاكُمْ}$$

"... so that you may not despair over matters that pass by, nor exult over favors bestowed upon you" (Qur'ān, 57:23).

Be informed that accepting what Allah Almighty decrees is the fruit of love for Allah, for when one loves something, he is pleased with what it does. A servant's pleasure with Allah is evidence of the pleasure of Allah Almighty with that servant: Such servants are pleased with Allah and they with him, and one who reaches such a status while Allah Almighty is pleased with him acquires the most perfect form of happiness and the most beautiful of all perfections: He remains relaxed because he does not tell himself that he wants this but not that: Both are the same, the Pleasure of Allah is the greatest of all; surely such is the most perfect form of wisdom. God willing, we will elaborate on this subject later in a chapter about acceptance with pleasure.

---

[40] This is narrated by Al-Sadūq in his *Tawhīd*, pp. 4, 337.

Be informed that weeping does not negate acceptance, nor does it incur wrath. Its source is the heart, as you will come to know by the will of Allah Almighty. Prophets and Imams, peace be with them, wept over their sons and loved ones; this is quite normal for humans, and there is no harm in it if it is not combined with anger as you will come to find out.

FIFTH

One afflicted with a calamity must consider the fact that he is living in an abode accustomed to toil and hardship; it is characterized by calamities and afflictions. What takes place in it is necessitated by its nature, and if the opposite takes place, it will be out of the ordinary especially to important personalities, men of nobility, prophets, successors to prophets and the righteous. All of whom have all suffered hardships and calamities too much for the mountains to carry as is well known in their biographies. If some of these are narrated, volumes will be needed.

The Prophet has said, "Those who are tried the most are the prophets then the righteous then the most exemplary."[41] And the Prophet has also said, "Life is the prison of the believer and the heaven of the unbeliever."[42]

---

[41] This is narrated by Al-Kolayni in his work *Al-Kāfi*, Vol. 2, pp. 2, 196, by Ibn Majah in his *Sunan*, Vol. 2, pp. 1334, 4023, by Al-Tirmidhi in his *Sunan*, Vol. 4, pp. 28, 2509, by Ahmed in his *Musnad*, Vol. 1, pp. 172, 180, 185, by Al-Darmi in his *Sunan*, Vol. 2, p. 320 and by Al-Hakim Al-Naishapuri in his *Mustadrak*, Vol. 1, p. 41 and Vol. 4, p. 307 with minor variation in wording.

[42] This tradition has been narrated by Al-Sadūq on p. 262, Vol. 4 of his work *Man la Yahdaruhu Al-Faqih*.

It has been said that there is no true pleasure in life; rather, its true pleasure is ease after pain. Its best pleasure is approaching women due to its result in getting progeny, yet how many pains would succeed it? The least pain is weakness, exhaustion from making a living and fatigue. Whenever something loved is acquired, it proves that the pain it incurs is more than the pleasure, and the happiness with it is not even one-tenth of the sighs it brings about. The least of its perils, in all reality, is parting with it which still causes pain to the heart and weakness to the body.

Any drink in life turns into mirage, any structure, no matter how good, is destined to ruin, any wealth, though an ignorant person is elated by it, will sooner or later vanish. Yet one who wades in deep waters never complains about wetness. One who enters between two ranks is not without fear, and how amazing is one who gets his hand into the snakes' mouths and complains about their stings! More amazing than him is one who expects a harmful thing to benefit him. One of the best speeches is the following by a man of virtue who eulogized his son's death by saying,

Its nature is polluted, yet you want it without impurities and pollutants,
One who expects days to be the opposite of their nature
Expects water to provide him with a torch.
If you wish for the impossible, you build on a crumbling cliff.

Some men of knowledge have said that one who is afflicted with a calamity ought to think of it as being less than what it is when he remembers that extinction is the ultimate end of all paths, that life is the abode of one who has no abode, the wealth of one who has no wealth. It is hoarded by one who is not rational, and it is sought by one who is not to be trusted. In it, those who have no knowledge become enemies of each other, those who do not deeply discern into things envy others who have it, those who are healthy become sick on its account, those who become sick because of it hate life, those who desire it out of want become grieved, and those who are enriched by it fall into trials and tribulations.

Be informed that you are created in this abode for a special purpose: Allah Almighty is above doing anything without a purpose; He has said, **"I have not created the jinns and mankind except so they may worship Me"** (Qur'ān, 51:56). He has made it an opportunity to win your way to eternity, making its rations the good deeds, its span the lifetime, which is very short compared to the sought eternal happiness which has no end.

If you work towards this end, if you remain vigilant as men do, if you care about it as the pious do, you will then hope to obtain your own share of its pleasures; so, do not waste your lifetime caring about anything other than the purpose for which this life is created for you; otherwise, you will then waste your time and consume your life without having benefited from it. One who goes never returns, a deceased man will never come back, and you will thus miss out on the [eternal] happiness for which you were created. Your sighs will then never end, your doing your own disservice will never alter, especially when you look and see the degrees earned by the righteous who race to do good, when you observe the stations of those who are close to Allah, and when you see how you fall short of doing acts of righteousness. Your store will be empty of profitable goods! Measure such pain and compare it with the worldly pains; shun away the hardest on you and the most harmful while you actually are capable of avoiding their root cause.

Imam Ali ﷺ has said, "If you are patient, destiny will be affected in your regard while you receive your rewards. And if you are impatient, destiny will be affected in your regard while you bear the weight of your sins[43]; so, take advantage of the opportunity of your youth before your old age, of your health before your illness, and let death stand before your eyes and get ready for it through good deeds; do not busy yourself watching someone for death is approaching you not the person." Contemplate on this verse of the Almighty:

وَأَنْ لَيْسَ لِلْإِنْسَانِ إِلَّا مَا سَعَىٰ ۞ وَأَنَّ سَعْيَهُ سَوْفَ يُرَىٰ

"Man can have nothing but what he strives for; (the fruit of) his striving will soon come in sight" (Qur'ān, 53:39-40).

So, do not be carried away too far with your hopes; reform your actions, for the main reason which prompts one to pay so much attention to wealth and sons is high hope.

The Prophet ﷺ has said to some of his companions, "When you receive the morning, do not talk to yourself about the evening, and when you are in the evening, do not talk to yourself about the morning: Take out from your life what benefits you in your death, from your health for your ailment, because you do not know what your name tomorrow will become."[44]

---

[43] *Nahjul-Balagha*, Vol. 3, pp. 291, 224.

[44] This tradition is narrated by Sheikh Waram in *Tanbih Al-Khatir*, Vol. 1, p. 271, by Sheikh Al-Tūsi in his Amāli, by Al-Daylami in his work *Irshād Al-Qulūb*, p. 18, and by Zaki ad-Deen in *Al-Targheeb wal Tarheeb*, Vol. 4, pp. 17, 243 with minor variation in wording.

Introduction

Imam Ali ﷺ has said, "The most concern I have about you are two characteristics: obeying desires and having high hopes. As for obeying desires, it takes one away from the path of righteousness. As for having high hopes, it brings about love for this life."[45] Then he said, "Allah grants life to whomsoever He likes or dislikes: But if He loves a servant of His, He grants him *imān*. Religion is served by some, and life is served by some; so, be among those who serve religion, and do not be among those who serve life. Indeed, life is leaving and the Hereafter is coming, and you are now in a life for action without reckoning, and you are about to approach a Day of Reckoning where there will be no deeds [to save you]."[46]

Be informed that a loved one who parts with you, so you stay feeling a sigh and a pain because of such parting, and if he is in touch with you, you labor, toil, work hard and exhaust yourself. Despite all of this, the time you spend with him is not without embittering through him or because of him so you may direct your mind away from him and seek another one to love: You will try hard to find him characterized by good health, continuous company, more pleasing and perfectly of benefit for you.

If you find such a person, he ought to be the one whom you seek and keep, about whom you care, with whom you spend your time, the ultimate love, the ultimate objective, and this is nothing other than keeping your mind occupied by Allah towards Whom you direct your attention, for such is love for Allah Almighty: He loves such folks and

---

[45] *Nahjul-Balagha*, Vol. 1, pp. 41, 88. It is also narrated by Al-Daylami from the Prophet ﷺ in *Irshād Al-Qublūb* with a minor wording variation.

[46] This is narrated by Al-Daylami from the Prophet ﷺ in *Irshād Al-Qublūb* with a minor wording variation.

they love Him, and those who have *imān* are the ones who love Allah the most.

The Prophet ﷺ has preconditioned love for Allah as a requirement of *imān* saying, "None of you truly believes till Allah and His Messenger are dearer to him than anyone else."⁴⁷ There can be no love for one whose actions are hated and with whom one is not pleased or when he himself is not actually pleased with such love.

Prophet Dawūd ؑ was once addressed by the Almighty ﷻ thus: "O David! Carry this message to those who live on My earth: I love those who love Me, I am the companion of those who accompany Me, the comfort for those who find comfort in remembering Me, the friend of those who befriend me. I choose those who choose Me, and I listen to those who obey Me. Nobody loves me truly from his heart except that I accept him for Myself and love him, too: None from among My creation is advanced over him. Whoever truly seeks me shall find Me, and whoever seeks anyone else shall never find Me. So, O people of the earth! Abandon your vain desires, and hurry towards My dignity, My company, My companionship: Feel comfortable about Me so I may give you comfort and hurry to loving you."⁴⁸

---

[47] This is recorded by Al-Faydh Al-Kashani in his work *Al-Mahajja Al-Baydhā'*, Vol. 8, p. 4. It is also narrated in a slightly different wording by Ahmed in his *Musnad*, Vol. 3, pp. 172, 248, by Al-Nisā'i in his *Sunan*, Vol. 8, p. 95 and by Ibn Majah in his *Sunan*, Vol. 2, pp. 1338, 4033.

[48] This is recorded by al-Majlisi in his *Bihār Al-Anwār*, Vol. 70, pp. 26, 28 and by Al-Hurr al-`Āmili in *Al-Jawāhir Al-Saniyya*, p. 94, where *Musakkin Al-Fuād* is quoted.

Allah The Almighty has inspired the following to one of the men of the truth: "There are among My servants those who love Me and whom I love. They are eager for Me and I for them. They remember Me and I remember them. If you follow your way, I shall love you, and if you avoid it, I shall hold you in contempt." The man of the truth asked, "Lord! What is their mark?" The Almighty said, "They look after their shadows during daylight just like a kind shepherd looks after his flock; they are eager for sunset just as the birds are eager for their nests at sunset. When night overshadows them, and when the dark settles, the beds are spread, and each lover seeks seclusion with the one whom he loves. They stand for Me on their feet [praying], facing the dust [in prostration], talking to Me silently through My own words, seeking to please Me by remembering My blessings upon them, some wailing and crying while others are sighing and complaining, some standing and sitting, while others are bowing and prostrating: I see with My eyes how they tolerate for My sake, and I hear how they complain about the love they have for Me in their hearts. The least that I give them are three things: first, I cast of My own *nūr* (light) into their hearts, so they talk about Me just as I talk about them; second, had the heavens and the earth and everything within been the weight of their deeds on the scale [of good deeds], I would have regarded that as too little for them; Third, I approach them with My face: One whom I approach with My face is one I know what he wants, so I give it to him."[49]

---

[49] This is recorded by al-Majlisi in his work *Bihār Al-Anwār*, Vol. 70, pp. 26, 28 where *Musakkin Al-Fuād* is quoted. It is also recorded by Al-Faydh Al-Kashani in *Al-Mahajja Al-Baydā'*, Vol. 8, p. 58.

Soothing the Heart of the Bereaved

1 - Rewards for the loss of children

Be informed that Allah, Praise to Him, is Just, Generous, and absolutely Independent. It does not befit His perfection and the beauty of His attributes that He afflicts one of His servants in the life of this world with any affliction, no matter how small, without rewarding him for it many times over. Had He not given him anything, He would have been unjust; and had He compensated him only by the same measure, He would have been sporting, and Allah is greatly above doing so. Many prophetic reports have supported each other in this regard; the following are only some of them:

"Had a believer known what rewards Allah ﷻ has prepared for him on account of his affliction, he would have wished he had been cut in the life of this world with scissors."[50]

Let us quote only what supports our topic, for such traditions have been narrated about the Prophet ﷺ by more than thirty of his companions.

---

[50] This tradition is recorded by Al-Kolayni in his book *Al-Kāfi*, Vol. 2, pp. 15, 198, by Al-Husayn ibn Sa`eed in his book *Al-Mu'min*, pp. 3, 15, by Sheikh Waram in *Tanbih Al-Khawatir*, Vol. 2, p. 204 and by Muhammed ibn Human in *Al-Tamhees*, pp. 13, 32, with variation in wording.

Al-Sadūq, may Allah have mercy on him, has narrated it through *isnad* to Amr ibn Absah al-Salami who said, "I heard the Messenger of Allah ﷺ saying, 'Any man offers three sons who did not yet reach maturity, or if a woman offers three of her sons, they will be a veil protecting him/her from the fire.'"[51]

Abu Dharr al-Ghifari, may Allah be pleased with him, has said, "There are no two Muslims [parents] who offer three sons who are yet to reach maturity except that Allah permits them to enter Paradise through His mercy."[52]

Through *isnad* (narration) by Jabir, traced back to Imam Abu Ja`far ibn Muhammed ibn Ali al-Baqir, peace be with them both, the Imam ﷺ said, "One who offers sons hoping for rewards from Allah Almighty will be protected from the Fire by the will of Allah, the most Exalted, the most Great."

Through *isnad* by Ali ibn Maysarah[53], Imam Abu Abdullah ﷺ says, "One son offered by a man is better than seventy who survive him, all having mounted over horses and fought in the Way of Allah."[54]

---

[51] *Thawab Al-A`mal*, pp. 2, 233.

[52] *Ibid*.

[53] His name is Ali ibn Maysrah ibn Abdullah Al-Nakh`i, their master, a man of Kufa. He and his father were companions of Imam Al-Sadiq ﷺ.

[54] This tradition is narrated by Al-Saduq who accepts it in his *Man la Yahduruhu Al- Faqih*, Vol. 1, pp. 112, 519 with variation in wording. It is also narrated by Al-Kolayni through his *isnad* to Isma`il Al-Sarraj in *Al-Kāfi*, Vol. 3, pp. 1, 218. It is also narrated by al-Tabrasi's grandson in *Mishkat Al-Anwar*,

1 - Rewards for the loss of children

He ﷺ is also cited as having said, "A believer's reward from his sons is Paradise, whether he was patient [at their demise] or not."[55] He ﷺ has also said, "If one is afflicted by a calamity, and if he fretted because of it or did not, whether he was patient about it or not, his reward from Allah for it will be Paradise."[56] He ﷺ has also said, "One son offered by a man is better for him than seventy who survive him and who live to meet al-Qaem, peace be with him."[57]

Al-Tirmidhi tracks his *isnad* the Prophet ﷺ saying, "A believer who is afflicted by a calamity in himself, his sons or wealth will meet Allah, the most Exalted, the most Great, having committed no sin at all."[58]

Muhammed ibn Khalid al-Salami, who cites his father quoting his grandfather, who used to keep the Prophet ﷺ company, said, "I heard the Messenger of Allah ﷺ saying, 'If a servant of Allah had a status with Allah which he did not achieve through a good deed, Allah afflicts him in his body, or in his wealth, or in the most dutiful of his sons, then He enables him to be patient on its account till he reaches the status which

---

p. 23, accepting its chain of narrators. It is also recorded by al-Majlisi in his *Bihar Al-Anwar*, Vol. 82, pp. 8, 116, where *Musakkin Al-Fuad* is quoted.

[55] This is narrated by Al-Saduq in his *Faqih*, Vol. 1, pp. 112, 518, by Al-Kolayni in his *Al-Kāfi*, Vol. 3, pp. 8, 219 and by *Bihar Al-Anwar*, Vol. 82, pp. 8, 116 from *Musakkin Al-Fuad*.

[56] *Man la Yahduruhu Al-Faqih*, Vol. 1, pp. 111, 517, *Bihar Al-Anwar*, Vol. 82, pp. 8, 116.

[57] *Thawab Al-A`mal*, pp. 4, 233.

[58] Al-Tirmidhi, *Sunan*, Vol. 4, pp. 28, 2510.

Allah, the most Exalted One, the most Great, had already decreed for him.'"⁵⁹

Thawbān, a servant-slave of the Messenger of Allah ﷺ, has said, "Congratulations! Congratulations! Five things there are: How heavy they are in the scales! They are: *La Ilaha illa Allah* [there is no god except Allah], *Subhan-Allah* (Glorified is Allah), *Alhamdu-Lillah* (Praise be to Allah), *Allahu Akbar* (Allah is Greatest), and the righteous son of a Muslim: He dies, so his father seeks compensation from Allah."⁶⁰

Abdul-Rahman ibn Samrah quotes the Messenger of Allah ﷺ as saying, "I saw yesterday something amazing," stating a lengthy tradition which includes this: "I saw a man from my nation whose scales were light, so his sons came and caused his scales to weigh down heavily."⁶¹

Sahl ibn Haneef, may Allah be pleased with him, has said that the Messenger of Allah ﷺ said, "Get married, for I shall brag about your numbers before the nations on the Judgment Day, so much so that the

---

⁵⁹ This tradition has been narrated by Abu Dawud in his *Sunan*, Vol. 3, pp. 183, 3090, by Ahmed in his *Musnad*, Vol. 5, p. 272, by Zaki ad-Deen in his book *Al-Targhib wal Tarhib*, Vol. 4, pp. 30, 283 and by Al-Suyuti in his book *Al-Jami` Al-Saghir*, Vol. 1, pp. 103, 669.

⁶⁰ Al-Saduq narrates it in his book Al-Khisal, Ahmed in his Mustadrak, Vol. 3, p. 443 and Vol. 4, pp. 5, 237 and Vol. 5, p. 366, Al-Hakim in his *Mustadrak*, Vol. 1, p. 511, Al-Suyuti in his *Al-Jami` Al-Saghir*, Vol. 1, pp. 483, 4129; and it is recorded by al-Majlisi in his *Bihar Al-Anwar*, Vol. 82, pp. 9, 117 from *Musakkin Al-Fuad*.

⁶¹ This is narrated by al-Suyuti in *Al-Jami` Al-Saghir*, Vol. 1, pp. 406, 2652, and it is recorded by al-Majlisi in his *Bihar Al-Anwar*, Vol. 82, 0. 117.

stillborn remains procrastinating at the gate of Paradise, so it is said to him to enter, but he says, 'Not before my parents enter.'"[62]

Mu`awiyah ibn Haidah al-Qushairi quotes the Prophet ﷺ as saying, "A slave woman who gives birth is better than a beautiful [free] woman who does not. I shall brag about your numbers before the nations, so much so that the stillborn will remain procrastinating at the gate of Paradise; therefore, it is said to him to enter Paradise, whereupon he would say, 'I and my parents?' and it will be said to him, 'You and your parents.'"[63]

Abdul-Malik ibn Omayr quotes narrators telling him that a man once went to the Prophet ﷺ and said, "O Messenger of Allah! Shall I marry so-and-so?" The Messenger of Allah ﷺ prohibited him from marrying her. He went to him a second time and said, "O Messenger of Allah! Shall I marry so-and-so?" The Messenger of Allah ﷺ prohibited him from marrying her, too. Then the man went to the Prophet ﷺ a third time, whereupon he ﷺ this time said to him, "A slave woman who gives birth is dearer to my heart than a beautiful [free] but sterile woman." Then he ﷺ added saying, "Do you not know that I shall brag about your numbers to the other nations? I shall do so till a stillborn remains at the gate of Paradise refusing to enter, so he is told to enter, but he says, 'No,

---

[62] This is narrated by Al-Saduq from Muhammed ibn Muslim from [Imam] Abu Abdullah ﷺ in *Al-Faqih*, Vol. 3, pp. 242, 1144, in *Ma`ani Al-Akhbar*, pp. 1, 291, and it is narrated by al-Tabrasi in *Makarim Al-Akhlaq*, p. 196, taking it for granted. It is also recorded by al-Majlisi in his *Bihar Al-Anwar*, Vol. 82, pp. 9, 117 from *Musakkin Al-Fuad*.

[63] This is narrated by Al-Suyuti in his book *Al-Jami` Al-Saghir*, Vol. 2, pp. 55, 4724 where he takes its authenticity for granted, and by Al-Muttaqi Al-Hindi who quotes Ibn Abbas in *Muntakhab Al-Kanz*, Vol. 6, p. 390.

not till my parents enter.' He thus seeks intercession for them, whereupon they shall all enter Paradise."

Sahl son of the Hanzali woman, who was childless and one of those who had sworn allegiance to the Prophet ﷺ under the tree, is quoted as having said, "If a son is born for me in Islam (who dies a stillborn), so I hope for compensation from Allah, is dearer to my heart than I have as my possession the whole world and everything in it."[64]

Ubadah ibn al-Samit is quoted as having said that the Messenger of Allah ﷺ had said, "A childbed woman is dragged by her son on the Judgment Day with his own naval cords into Paradise [the child died before getting the chance to cut the naval cord]."[65]

Amr ibn Shu`ayb quotes his father quoting his grandfather saying that the Messenger of Allah ﷺ had said, "Whoever offers one son from his loins, who is yet to reach adolescence, it will be better for him than a hundred sons who survive him, all performing *jihad* in the cause of Allah who never are calmed till Judgment Day."

---

[64] This is narrated by Ibn Al-Athīr in *Usd Al-Ghāba*, Vol. 2, p. 364 and by Al-Muttaqi Al-Hindi in *Muntakhab Al-Kanz*, Vol. 6, p. 392 with minor wording variation.

[65] This tradition is narrated by Ahmed in his *Musnad*, Vol. 3, p. 489 and Vol. 5, p. 329. It is narrated by Muhammed ibn Ali al-Alawi through another *isnad* on pp. 25, 53 of *Al-Ta`azi* and by al-Majlisi in *Bihar Al-Anwar*, Vol. 82, pp. 10, 117 from *Musakkin Al-Fuad*.

Al-Hasan has said that the Messenger of Allah ﷺ said, "If I offer a stillborn, it is better for me than leaving behind a hundred knights, all fighting in the cause of Allah."[66]

The Prophet ﷺ is also quoted as having said, "Stillborns will be told on the Judgment Day to enter Paradise, whereupon they will say, 'Lord! Not till our parents enter!' They will thus refuse to enter. It is then that the Almighty, Exalted and Great is He, shall say, 'Why do I see you hesitating? Enter Paradise.' They will say, 'Lord! Our parents!' The Almighty will then say, 'Enter Paradise, you and your parents.'"[67]

Ubaid ibn Umayr al-Laithi is quoted as having said, "On the Judgment Day, the sons of the Muslims will come out of Paradise holding drinks in their hands. People will beg them to give them of it to drink, but they will shout out: 'Our parents! [Where are] our parents?!' so much so that even the stillborn will remain at the gate of Paradise too reluctant to enter saying, 'I shall not enter till my parents enter.'"[68]

Anas ibn Malik is quoted as having cited the Messenger of Allah ﷺ saying, "When it is Judgment Day, the believers' children are called upon to get out of their graves. They will come out. They will then be told to go to Paradise in hordes, but they will say, 'Lord! Shall our parents accompany us?' They will be called upon a second time to go to Paradise in hordes, but they will again say, 'Lord! Shall our parents accompany us?' They will then be called upon for the third time to go to Paradise in hordes, but they will once more say, 'Lord! What about

---

[66] *Tanbih Al-Khawatir*, Vol. 1, p. 287; *Al-Mahajja Al-Baydaa*, Vol. 8, p. 287.
[67] This is narrated by Ahmed in his *Musnad*, Vol. 4, p. 105.
[68] This is recorded by al-Majlisi in his book *Bihar Al-Anwar*, Vol. 82, pp. 11, 118 where he cites *Musakkin Al-Fuad*.

our parents?' It will be said to them on the fourth time, 'Your parents shall be with you, too,' whereupon each child will leap to its parents. They will take their hands, and all will enter Paradise, for they best know their fathers and mothers on that Day than your own sons who now are in your homes."[69]

Anas ibn Malik is quoted as having said that a man used to bring his son together with him whenever he used to see the Messenger of Allah. The son died, so his father stopped going to visit the Prophet who inquired about him. People said to the Prophet, "O Messenger of Allah! His son, whom you had seen in his company, has died." The Prophet said, "Why did you not tell me? Stand and let us go to our brother to console him." When the Prophet entered the man's place, he found him very sad and forlorn, so he offered his condolences to him. The man said, "O Messenger of Allah! I used to treasure him for my old age and feebleness." The Messenger of Allah said to him, "Does it not please you that on the Day of Judgment, he will be beside you? He will be told to enter Paradise, whereupon he will say, 'Lord! What about my parents?' He will keep pleading till Allah, the most Exalted, the most Great, accepts his intercession and permits you all to enter Paradise."[70]

Anas is also quoted as having said that Uthman ibn Maz`un, may Allah be pleased with him, lost a son; therefore, his grief was intense, so much so that he took for himself a niche in his house where he worshipped. The Prophet came to know about it, whereupon he said, "O Uthman!

---

[69] *Ibid.*, Vol. 82, p. 118 from *Musakkin Al-Fuad* where Anas ibn Malik is quoted.

[70] This is recorded by al-Majlisi in his book *Bihar Al-Anwar*, Vol. 82, p. 118 from *Musakkin Al-Fuad*.

Allah, the most Exalted One, the most Great, did not obligate us to live like monks. Rather, asceticism of my nation is *jihad* (holy war) in the way of Allah. O Uthman son of Maz`un! Paradise has eight gates and Hell has seven; does it not please you that whenever you come to any gate of Paradise, you will find your son standing at it, holding your robe (pleading to the Almighty to let you in)?" It was said to the Messenger of Allah ﷺ, "O Messenger of Allah! Shall we get with regard to our sons what Uthman will be getting?" The Prophet ﷺ said, "Yes, for all those among you who are patient and who rest their hope on Allah's rewards."[71]

Qurrah ibn Iyas is quoted as having said that the Prophet ﷺ used to be visited by a man from the Ansār with his son. The Prophet ﷺ once asked him, "O so-and-so! Do you love him?" The man said, "Yes, O Messenger of Allah, I love him just as I love you." The Prophet ﷺ missed seeing him, so he asked about him. It was said to him, "O Messenger of Allah! He lost his son." When the Prophet ﷺ saw that man again, he said to him, "Are you not pleased that on the Judgment Day, whenever you come to one of the gates of Paradise, your son will try to open it for you?" The man said, "O Messenger of Allah! Will the gate be opened only for him or for all of us [our family]?" The Prophet ﷺ said, "Rather, for all of you."[72]

---

[71] This is reported by al-Saduq's book *Al-Amali*, by Muhammed ibn Ali al-Alawi in his *Al-Ta`āzi*, pp. 16, 28, and it is reported by Ibn al-Fattal, the Persian, in *Rawdat Al-Wā`izeen*, p. 422, with minor difference in wording.

[72] This is reported by Muhammed ibn Ali in his book *Al-Ta`āzi*, pp. 14, 24, by Ahmed in his *Musnad*, by al-Nisā'i in his *Sunan*, Vol. 4, p. 23, by al-Hakim al-Naishapuri in his *Mustadrak*, Vol. 1, p. 384, by al-Suyuti in *Al-Durr Al-Manthur*, Vol. 1, p. 158, and by Zaki ad-Deen in *Al-Targheeb wal Tarheeb*, Vol. 3, pp. 16, 79.

Al-Bayhaqi has reported that whenever the Prophet ﷺ sat, a number of his companions would sit around him, and among them was a father who had with him a small boy who used to come to him from behind, so he would seat him in front of him, till the child died, whereupon the man stopped going to the circle which he used to attend due to his sadness and grief. He was missed by the Prophet ﷺ who said, "Why do I not see so-and-so?" They said, "O Messenger of Allah! His son whom you had seen has died, so he now is too grieving over him to attend." The Prophet ﷺ met him and asked him about his son. He told the Prophet ﷺ about his son's demise, so the Prophet ﷺ offered his condolences to him then said, "O so-and-so! Which is dearer to you: That you enjoy him during your life, or you come tomorrow to one of the gates of Paradise where you will find him there ready to open it for you?" The man said, "O Prophet of Allah! No, indeed, I prefer he beats me to the gate of Paradise which is dearer to me." The Prophet ﷺ said, "You shall have that."[73] A man from among the Ansār stood up and said, "Is this [reward] only for this man or is it for anyone from among the Muslims who has a child [who passes away]?" The Prophet ﷺ said, "Rather, it is for anyone among the Muslims who has a child [who passes away]; he shall have the same [rewards]."

Zurarah ibn Awfa is quoted as having said that the Messenger of Allah ﷺ consoled a man on the loss of his son. He said to him, "Allah will reward you, and great will be His reward." The man said, "O Messenger of Allah! I am an old man, and my son had tended to me very well." The Prophet ﷺ said to him, "Does it not please you that he will meet you at one of the gates of Paradise with a drink in his hand for you?" The man asked, "How can I get such a reward, O Messenger of Allah?!"

---

[73] It is narrated by Nisā'i in his *Sunan*, Vol. 4, p. 118 with minor wording difference.

The Prophet ﷺ said, "Allah will take care of it and will do the same to every Muslim whose son dies in Islam."

Abdullah ibn Qays quotes the Messenger of Allah ﷺ saying, "If the son of a servant of Allah dies, Allah Almighty says this to His angels: 'Have you taken away the son of My servant?' He will receive the answer in the affirmative, whereupon He will repeat the question thus: 'Have you taken away the fruit of his heart?' The angels will again answer in the affirmative, whereupon He will ask them—and He knows in advance what their answer will be—this: 'What did My servant say?' They will answer saying, 'He praised You and rendered his final affair to You.' Allah Almighty will then say, 'Build a house for My servant in Paradise and name it the House of Praise.'"[74]

It has also been narrated that a woman came once to see the Prophet ﷺ in the company of her sick son. She said, "O Messenger of Allah! Pray Allah Almighty to heal my son!" The Messenger of Allah ﷺ said to her, "Did you have [other] children?" She said, "Yes". He asked her, "Were they born during the *jahiliyya* or in Islam?" She said, "during Islam."

---

[74] This is narrated by al-Kolayni the *isnad* of which he refers to al-Sikūni from Imam Abu Abdullah ؑ from the Prophet ﷺ, and it is also narrated in *Al-Kāfi*, Vol. 3, pp. 4, 218, by al-Saduq in Vol. 1, pp. 112, 523 of *Al-Faqih* with a variation in its wording. It is also narrated from Abu Musa al-Ash`ari by Ahmed in his *Musnad*, Vol. 4, p. 415 and by al-Suyuti in his *Al-Jami` Al-Saghīr*, Vol. 1, pp. 131, 854. It is also recorded by al-Majlisi in his *Bihar Al-Anwar*, Vol. 82, p. 119 from *Musakkin Al-Fuad*.

The Messenger of Allah ﷺ said, "[Such is] a fortified protection [from the fire of hell]! A fortified protection!"[75]

Jabir ibn Samrah is quoted as having said that the Messenger of Allah ﷺ had said, "One who buries three of his sons and is patient about his loss and rests his hope on being compensated for his loss by Allah Almighty, it will be incumbent that he should be lodged in Paradise." Umm Ayman asked, "What if he buries two?" The Prophet ﷺ said, "It is so if he buries two and is patient about his loss and rests his hope on being compensated for his loss by Allah Almighty, it will be incumbent that he should be lodged in Paradise." Umm Ayman asked again, "What about burying only one son?" The Prophet took to silence. After a short while he said, "O Umm Ayman! If someone buries one son and is patient about his loss and rests his hope on being compensated for his loss by Allah Almighty, it will be incumbent that he should be lodged in Paradise."[76]

Abdullah ibn Mas`ūd, may Allah be pleased with him, is quoted as having said that the Messenger of Allah ﷺ had said, "If one offers three sons who were yet to reach adolescence, they will be his fortified protection [against the flames of the Fire]." Abu Dharr said, "I have already offered two." The Prophet ﷺ said, "Even if they were two."

---

[75] This is recorded by al-Majlisi on pp. 12, 119 of Vol. 82 from *Musakkin Al-Fuad*.

[76] This tradition is narrated by al-Suyuti in *Al-Durr Al-Manthur*, Vol. 1, p. 159, and in *Al-Jami` Al-Kabeer*, Vol. 1, p. 777 with a difference in wording. It is also recorded by al-Majlisi in his *Bihar Al-Anwar*, Vol. 82, pp. 12, 119 from *Musakkin Al-Fuad*.

Ubayy ibn Ka`b then said, "I have offered one," whereupon the Prophet ﷺ said, "Even if it were one son, but this will be at the first shock."[77]

Abu Sa`eed al-Khudri is quoted as having said that women once said this to the Prophet ﷺ: "Schedule one day to preach to us." He did. He said, "Any woman who loses three of her children, they will all form a barrier for her to protect her from the fire." One woman asked him, "What about a woman who loses two?" The Prophet ﷺ said, "It is so even if she loses two."[78]

In another tradition, he ﷺ said to her, "Do you not like to see him at the gate of Paradise calling upon you to join us?" She answered in the affirmative, so he ﷺ said to her, "So shall it be."[79]

Ubayy ibn al-Nadhar al-Salami is quoted as having said that the Messenger of Allah ﷺ had said, "If one of the Muslims loses three of his children and he rests his hope on compensations from Allah ﷻ, they

---

[77] Ahmed has narrated this tradition in his *Musnad*, Vol. 1, p. 429, and so has Al-Tirmidhi in his *Sunan*, Vol. 2, pp. 262, 1067, Ibn Majah in his *Sunan*, Vol. 1, pp. 512, 1066 and Al-Suyuti in *Al-Durr Al-Manthur*, Vol. 1, p. 158.

[78] This tradition is narrated by Muhammed ibn Ali in *Al-Ta`azi*, Vol. 13, p. 21 with a wording variation. It is also narrated by Ahmed in his *Musnad*, Vol. 3, p. 34, by Al-Bukhari in his *Sahih*, Vol. 1, pp. 2, 9, 36, 124 with some wording variation. It is also narrated by Muslim in his *Sahih*, Vol. 4, pp. 2028, 2632 from Abu Hurayra and by Zaki ad-Deen in *Al-Targheeb wal Tarheeb*, Vol. 3, p. 76 with a wording variation.

[79] This is narrated by Al-Muttaqi Al-Hindi in *Muntakhab Kanzul-`Ummal*, Vol. 1, p. 212 with some wording variation and by Al-Majlisi in his *Bihar Al-Anwar*, Vol. 82, p. 120 from *Musakkin Al-Fuad*.

will be protection for him against the fire." A woman asked, "What if two die?" The Prophet ﷺ said, "Even if he/she loses two."

He ﷺ is also quoted as having said, "One who offers three of his children while being patient and seeks compensations from Allah ﷻ, he will be protected from the Fire by the will of Allah, the most Exalted One, the most Great."[80]

In another wording of this tradition, the Prophet ﷺ says, "One who loses some of his sons and remains patient, seeking compensations from Allah ﷻ, they will protect him, by the will of Allah, from the Fire."[81]

The mother of Mubashshir, who belongs to the Ansar, is quoted as saying that the Messenger of Allah ﷺ entered her house as she was cooking rice. He said to her, "One who loses three children who are yet to reach adolescence will be protected through them from the Fire." She said to him, "O Messenger of Allah! What about one who loses only two?" He said to her, "It shall be so even if he loses two children, O mother of Mubashshir!"[82]

Qabeesah ibn Barmah has said, "I was once sitting in the company of the Prophet ﷺ when a woman came to him and said, 'O Messenger of Allah! Pray to Allah! Pray to Allah for my sake, for no son lives for me.'

---

[80] This is narrated by Sheikh Waram in *Tanbih Al-Khawatir*, Vol. 1, p. 287 where its authenticity is taken for granted. It is also narrated from Abu Al-Nadar by Malik ibn Anas in his *Muwatta'*, Vol. 1, p. 235, and by Al-Suyuti in *Al-Durr Al-Manthur*, Vol. 1, p. 158.

[81] *Al-Jami` Al-Kabeer*, Vol. 1, p. 817.

[82] This is narrated by Al-Suyuti in *Al-Jami` Al-Kabeer*, Vol. 1, p. 949 with a wording variation.

The Prophet ﷺ asked her, 'How many sons have you lost?' She said, 'Three'. He said, 'Surely you have been protected from the Fire with a strong protection.'"[83]

Ubayy ibn Ka`b is quoted as having said that the Prophet ﷺ once asked a woman if she had children. "Three", she said. The Prophet ﷺ said, "This is a fortified protection for you."

The Prophet ﷺ is also quoted as having said, "Whenever two Muslims [husband and wife] offer three [children] who are yet to reach adolescence, Allah ﷻ will lodge them in Paradise through His mercy." People said to him, "O Messenger of Allah! What if only two are offered?" He said, "Even if they offer two; there are some people in my nation who enter Paradise through his intercession more than [the tribe of] Mudar's count, and there are others who work so hard for Hell till they become one of its corners."[84] A group of narrators have reported this tradition, labeling it as authentic.

He ﷺ has also said, "Allah Almighty has said, 'My Love is deserved by those who befriend each other for My sake, and my Love is due to those

---

[83] This tradition has been reported by Ibn al-Athīr in *Usd Al-Ghaba*, Vol. 4, p. 191, and it is transmitted from Abu Hurayra with variation in its wording by Ahmed in his *Musnad*, Vol. 2, p. 419 and by Muslim in his *Sahih*, Vol. 4, p. 2030.

[84] This is narrated by Al-Hakimal-Naishapuri in *Al-Mustadrak*, Vol. 1, p. 71 and by Zaki ad-Deen in *Al-Targheeb wal Tarheeb*, Vol. 3, pp. 12, 78. It is narrated by Ahmed in his *Musnad* in different wording in Vol. 4, p. 212 and Vol. 5, 312.

who help each other for My sake."⁸⁵ Then he said, "A believing man or woman who loses [to death] three children from his loins who did not yet reach adolescence [and who rests his hope on rewards from Allah] will be lodged into Paradise through Allah's ﷻ mercy for those whom he loses."⁸⁶

The Prophet ﷺ is also quoted as having said, "One who buries three of his children, Allah will prohibit the Fire from reaching him."⁸⁷

Sa`sa`ah ibn Mu`awiyah is quoted as having said, "I met Abu Dharr al-Ghifari, may Allah be pleased with him, in the Rabadha with a camel on which he had loaded two bags, and on the camel's neck he was hanging a water bag. I said to him, 'O Abu Dharr! What is wrong?!' He said, 'I am just working.' I said to him, 'Narrate a tradition for me, may Allah have mercy on you.' He said, 'I heard the Messenger of Allah ﷺ say that any Muslim couple whose three children die before reaching the age of maturity will be forgiven by Allah through the favor of His mercy on account of those whom they lose.'" He went on to ask Abu Dharr to tell him another tradition, whereupon Abu Dharr al-Ghifari said, "I heard the Messenger of Allah ﷺ say, 'If a Muslim spends in the way of Allah a couple of items, the caretakers of Paradise will all call upon him to take what belongs to him.' I asked him, 'How so?' He ﷺ said, 'If he had offered men, they will be doubled for him, if

---

⁸⁵ Ahmed has narrated it in his *Musnad*, Vol. 4, p. 386 and Zaki ad-Deen in *Al-Targheeb wal Tarheeb*, Vol. 4, pp. 16, 19 with minor wording variation.
⁸⁶ This is narrated by al-Nisa'i in his *Sunan*, Vol. 4, p. 34 with minor wording difference and by al-Muttaqi Al-Hindi in *Muntakhab Al-Kanz*, Vol. 1, p. 210 with different wording.
⁸⁷ This is narrated by al-Suyuti in *Al-Jami` Al-Sagheer*, Vol. 2, pp. 600, 8669 and by al-Muttaqi al-Hindi in *Muntakhab Al-Kanz*, Vol. 1, p. 210.

camels, cattle, etc., these will be doubled for him, too,' counting all species of sacrificial animals."[88] This tradition is mentioned by a group of narrators.

Anas ibn Malik has said that the Messenger of Allah ﷺ stood in a congregation of Banu Salamah and said, "O sons of Salamah! How would you describe a childless person among you?" They said, "He [or she] is one who does not have children." He ﷺ said, "Rather, he is one for whom no children are born." He ﷺ asked them again, "How would you describe a destitute among you?" They said, "He is one who has no wealth." The Prophet ﷺ said, "No, he is one who meets his Maker having done nothing good for His sake."[89]

Ibn Mas`ūd is quoted as having said that the Messenger of Allah ﷺ visited a woman once to offer his condolences. He said to her, "It has come to my knowledge that you became very grieved." She said, "What would prevent me, O Messenger of Allah, from it since he [son who died] has left me a childless old woman?" The Messenger of Allah ﷺ said to her, "You are not childless. A childless woman is one who dies without having begotten sons and people cannot get their sons to help her; such is the childless woman."

All these traditions are excerpted from reliable sources. We have left out their *isnad* and sources for the sake of brevity, and due to the fact that Allah, the most Praised One, through His favor and mercy, has promised rewards for those who do their best to achieve something even

---

[88] This is narrated by Ahmed in his *Musnad*, Vol. 5, pp. 151, 153, 159, 164 with minor wording difference.

[89] This is narrated by al-Suyuti in *Al-Jami` Al-Kabeer*, Vol. 1, p. 959 with minor wording variation.

if they do not actually achieve it. The same is recorded by books of traditions from our [Shiite] sources and from those of the majority of Muslims [Jama'a].

More on rewards for loss of children from other sources

Zaid ibn Aslam is quoted as having said that Prophet David, peace be with him, lost a son, so he grieved a great deal for him. Allah ﷻ, therefore, inspired this to him: "O David! What was the worth of this son for you?" He said, "Lord! He was equal to the fill of the earth with gold." The Almighty said, "Then you will have from Me on the Day of Judgment as many rewards as would fill this earth."[90]

Dawūd ibn Abu Hind is quoted as having said that he saw in a vision once as if it was Doomsday and people were called upon for reckoning. He said, "I was brought closer to the scales: My good deeds were placed on one scale and my sins were put on the other. The scale of sins weighed heavier than that of the good deeds. As I stood very upset about it, I was brought a white handkerchief or rag on which I placed my good deeds, thus the scale of my good deeds weighed heavier. I was asked, 'Do you know what this [rag] is?' I answered in the negative. It was said to me, 'This was a stillborn begotten for you.' I said, 'I had a daughter.' It was said to me, 'Such was not your daughter because you wished she would die.'"

Abu Shawdhab has said that a man had a son who was yet to reach the age of adolescence. He sent a message to his folks that he needed something. When asked about it, he said, "I want to implore Allah Almighty to take away the life of this son of mine, and I want you to say 'Amen' to it." They asked him why he wanted to do that. He told them that he had seen in a vision as though people were gathered for the Judgment Day, and they were very thirsty. Boys came out of

---

[90] This is narrated by Sheikh *Waram in Tanbih Al-Khawatir*, Vol. 1, p. 287 and by al-Suyuti in *Al-Durr Al-Manthur*, Vol. 5, p. 306 in different wording.

Paradise carrying water jugs, and among them was one of his nephews. He asked his nephew to give him a drink, but he refused and said, 'O uncle! We give only our fathers to drink.' I, therefore, liked Allah ﷻ to count my son among them." He supplicated, and they kept saying "Amen" till the boy died. This is recorded by al-Bayhaqi in *Al-Shu`ab*.

Muhammed ibn Khalaf is quoted as having said, "Ibrahim al-Harbi had a son who was eleven years old and who had learned the text of the Holy Qur'ān by heart. His father had taught him a good deal of *fiqh* and *hadith*. His son died, so I went to offer my condolences. He said to me, 'I was hoping he would die.' I said to him, 'O father of Ishaq! You are the world's scholar, why do you still talk like that about a son whom you begot then taught *hadith* and *fiqh*?!' He said, 'Yes, even so. I saw in a vision as though it was Doomsday. Young boys were carrying water jars and were serving people water, and the day was terribly hot. I asked one of them to give me of that water. He looked at me and said that I was not his father. I asked him who they all were, and he said that they were children who died during the past life, leaving their parents behind, and that they now were receiving them and serving them water. This is why I wished that he would die.'"[91]

In his book titled *Al-Ihyaa*, al-Ghazali narrates saying that there was a particular righteous man to whom marriage was suggested a number of times, but he always refused. One day he woke up from his sleep and asked others to help him get married. He was asked about his sudden change of heart, so he said, "I hope perhaps the Almighty will grant me a son then take him away so he will be in the Hereafter in the forefront." Then he said, "I saw in my vision as if the Day of Judgment had approached. It was as though I was among the crowds in that situation

---

[91] *Rijal Al-Hadith*, Vol. 16, p. 74; *Khulasat Al-`Alama*, Vol. 1, pp. 154, 161.

suffering from thirst that would tear my heart apart, and so were the rest of beings because of thirst and hardship. As we were thus, boys made their way in the midst of people carrying lanterns of *nūr* (celestial light) and also carrying water jars made of silver and cups made of gold. They gave water to one person after the other. They were going through the crowds, bypassing most of them by. I stretched my hand to one of them and said to him, "Give me a drink for thirst has worn me out.' He said, 'You have no son among us; we only give drink to our parents.' I asked him, 'Who are you?' He said, 'We are children of Muslim parents who died.'"[92]

Sheikh Abu Abdullah ibn al-Nu`man, in his book *Musbah al-Zalam*, quotes some trustworthy persons saying that a man asked a friend of his who was going to perform the pilgrimage to convey his greetings to the Messenger of Allah ﷺ and to bury a sealed tablet which he gave him at his sacred head. The man did so. When the friend returned, the man was generous to him and said, "May Allah reward you with goodness! You have conveyed the message!" The pilgrim was surprised at how his friend came to know about what he had done, so he asked his friend, "How did you know that I had conveyed the message before I even opened my mouth to talk to you about it?!" He started explaining to him by saying, "I had a brother who died, leaving a small son whom I brought up well, then he, too, died before reaching adolescence. One night, I saw in a vision that Judgment Day had come, and the Gathering had taken place. People were extremely thirsty on account of their exertion. My nephew had water in his hand, so I begged him to give me of it, but he refused and said, 'My father deserves it more than you.' This hit me hard, so I woke up terrified. In the morning, I paid some dinars by way of charity and prayed to Allah to grant me a son, and He

---

[92] *Ihyaa Uloom ad-Dīn*, Vol. 2, p. 27.

did. Your trip came, so I wrote that sheet which contained a plea to the Prophet ﷺ to accept my son in the hope I will find him on the Day of the Great Fright. He had a fever which ended his life, and this took place on the day of your arrival; therefore, I knew that you had conveyed the message."

In the book titled *Al-Nawm wal Ru'ya*, Abu al-Saqr al-Musilli says, "Ali son of al-Husain son of Ja`far says that his father has been told by some of our fellows, those whose creed and comprehension he trusts, that he came to Medina once in the evening and slept in the Baqi` between four graves where there was a freshly dug up grave. I saw in my vision four children coming out of those graves reciting these verses of poetry:

'Allah has blessed us with seeing the Loved One,
With your own coming, O Umaim, to us!
Never did I wonder about the grave's pressure
And about your coming, O Umaim, to us together!'

So, I told myself that these verses must surely have some meaning. I stayed there till sunrise. It was then that a coffin was brought. I asked whose coffin it was, and I was told that it belonged to a female resident of Medina. I said, 'Is her name Umaima?' They said, 'Yes'. I said, 'Has she lost [to death] some of her sons?' They said, 'Four sons,' whereupon I told them about what I knew, and this only increased their puzzlement."[93]

How good are these verses by some men of virtue?

I give him when he gives me, pleasure,

---

[93] Al-Majlisi, *Bihar Al-Anwar*, Vol. 82, p. 122.

1 - Rewards for the loss of children

And if He takes away what He gives me He rewards:
Which of these blessings shall I regard to be better?
And for which shall I count as the most rewarding upon the Return?

Soothing the Heart of the Bereaved

2 - Patience and its aftermath

In language, patience means one restraining himself during periods of panic about something the advent of which is hated and about fretting on its account. This takes place when one prevents his inner self from being perturbed, his parts from unusual motion, and it falls into three types:

FIRST: General patience: Self-restraint as a way for showing forbearance and demonstrating firmness during trials and tribulations so people will be regarded by men of reason and by the general public as accepting whatever comes up in the life of this world while being unaware of the advent of the Hereafter.[94]

SECOND: Patience of the ascetics, the true worshippers, the men of piety, the men of clemency, due to their expecting rewards for it in the Hereafter; surely those who persevere will be granted their rewards without count.[95]

---

[94] This is the meaning derived from 30:7 of the Holy Qur'an.

[95] This meaning is derived from the Holy Qur'an, 39:10.

THIRD: Patience of the Gnostics, for some of them are pleased when something hated takes place to them due to their belief that the One Whom they adore has singled them out for it from among all other people, so they have become recognized (by the honor of His having cast a look at them):

$$وَبَشِّرِ الصَّابِرِينَ ۞ الَّذِينَ إِذَا أَصَابَتْهُم مُّصِيبَةٌ قَالُوا إِنَّا لِلَّهِ وَإِنَّا إِلَيْهِ رَاجِعُونَ ۞ أُولَٰئِكَ عَلَيْهِمْ صَلَوَاتٌ مِّن رَّبِّهِمْ وَرَحْمَةٌ ۖ وَأُولَٰئِكَ هُمُ الْمُهْتَدُونَ$$

> "... Give glad tidings to those who patiently persevere and, when afflicted with calamity, say, 'To Allah do we belong, and to Him do we return'. They are the ones on whom God's blessings and mercy (descend), and they are the ones who receive guidance" (Qur'ān, 2:155-157).

This type is exclusively relevant to accepting whatever the Almighty decrees, and we will discuss it in a special chapter.

The first type has no rewards in it because it is not done for the sake of Allah ﷻ. Rather, it is done for the sake of people; it is in reality mere pretension: Everything said about pretension applies to it. But impatience is worse because human souls incline to emulate their peers, the ones with whom they mix, they like, so they would thus disseminate patience among them. If they see the conditions of those who persevere, their souls will incline to emulate their norms of conduct, and this may become a cause for their perfection and thus benefit may be reaped in the same type of system even if the persevering person himself may not be perfect.

Patience, in the absolute sense, is applied to the second type. Be informed that Allah, the most Praised One, has described the patient ones, mentioning those who persevere in the Qur'ān in more than seventy places, attaching many good things and degrees to patience and to making them its fruit:

The greatest One has said:

$$\text{وَجَعَلْنَا مِنْهُمْ أَئِمَّةً يَهْدُونَ بِأَمْرِنَا لَمَّا صَبَرُوا ۖ وَكَانُوا بِآيَاتِنَا يُوقِنُونَ}$$

"And We appointed leaders from among them, giving guidance under Our command so long as they persevered with patience and continued to believe in Our Signs" (Qur'ān, 32:24).

He has also said,

$$\text{وَتَمَّتْ كَلِمَتُ رَبِّكَ الْحُسْنَىٰ عَلَىٰ بَنِي إِسْرَائِيلَ بِمَا صَبَرُوا}$$

"The fair promise of your Lord was fulfilled for the Children of Israel because they had patience and constancy" (Qur'ān, 7:137).

The Almighty has also said,

$$\text{وَلَنَجْزِيَنَّ الَّذِينَ صَبَرُوا أَجْرَهُم بِأَحْسَنِ مَا كَانُوا يَعْمَلُونَ}$$

"And We will certainly bestow rewards on those who patiently persevere according to the best of their deeds" (Qur'ān, 16:96).

He has also said,

$$\text{أُولَٰئِكَ يُؤْتَوْنَ أَجْرَهُم مَّرَّتَيْنِ بِمَا صَبَرُوا}$$

"Twice will they be given their reward because they have persevered" (Qur'ān, 28:54).

He has also said,

$$\text{إِنَّمَا يُوَفَّى الصَّابِرُونَ أَجْرَهُم بِغَيْرِ حِسَابٍ}$$

"Those who patiently persevere will indeed receive their reward without measure!" (Qur'ān, 39:10).

Every sacrifice has its own reward according to a measure and a calculation except perseverance. Since fasting is derived from perseverance, and since it is equivalent to half of perseverance[96], rewards for it are handled only by Allah, the most Praised One, the most Exalted, as books of traditions tell us.

Allah Almighty has said [in a Qudsi *hadith*]: "Fasting is for My sake, and I am the One Who rewards for it."[97] Thus, He added it to Himself

---

[96] This is recorded by Ibn Majah in his *Sunan*, Vol. 1, pp. 555, 1745 and in al-Suyuti's *Al-Jami` Al-Saghir*, Vol. 2, pp. 122, 5200 in a chapter titled "Fast is half perseverance".

[97] This is narrated by al-Saduq in *Al-Khisal*, pp. 42, 45, by Malik in *Al-Muwatta'*, Vol. 1, pp. 58, 310, by al-Bukhari in his *Sahih*, Vol. 3, p. 31 and by Ibn Majah in his *Sunan*, Vol. 2, pp. 1256, 3823. Ibn al-Athīr says the following in his *Al-Nihaya*, Vol. 1, p. 270 after mentioning this text: "Many have interpreted this tradition, saying that He did not specify fasting for His own rewards, the most Exalted One, the most Great, that He is, although all acts of adoration are for His sake and their rewards come from Him. They have stated many viewpoints about it all of which revolve round the fast being a

from among all other acts of worship, promising those who persevere that He is with them, saying,

وَاصْبِرُوا ۚ إِنَّ اللَّهَ مَعَ الصَّابِرِينَ
"... And persevere, for Allah is with those who persevere" (Qur'ān, 8:46),

hinging His support on perseverance and saying,

---

secret between Allah and His servant with which nobody is acquainted except Him. No servant of Allah is truly fasting except if he is sincere in his desire to obey the Almighty. They have also said that acts of adoration besides fasting share the latter in the secret of obedience such as one performing his prayers without being cleansed of impurity or in a garment which is polluted with impurity and other such secrets related to acts of adoration with which only Allah and their performer are familiar. The best that I have heard in interpreting this tradition is that all acts of adoration are meant to seek nearness to Allah Almighty such as prayers, pilgrimage, charity, i`tikaf (solitude in mosque), tabattul (supplication), hadi (sacrifice) and other types of adorations: The polytheists had performed them as they worshipped their gods and whatever they used as partners with Allah, yet nobody ever heard that a sect among the polytheists and followers of a creed worshipped their gods through fasting nor sought nearness to them through its medium, nor has fasting ever been associated with acts of worship save when it is part of Shari'a (law). For this reason, the Almighty has said: "Fasting is for My sake, and I am the One Who rewards for it," that is, "Nobody is a partner with Me in it, nor has anyone been adored through it save Me: I, therefore, am the One Who rewards for it on My own; I do not let anyone else do so be he an angel close to Me or anyone else regardless of how close he is to Me."

بَلَىٰ ۚ إِن تَصْبِرُوا وَتَتَّقُوا وَيَأْتُوكُم مِّن فَوْرِهِمْ هَٰذَا يُمْدِدْكُمْ رَبُّكُم بِخَمْسَةِ آلَافٍ مِّنَ الْمَلَائِكَةِ مُسَوِّمِينَ

"Yes, if you remain firm and act rightly, even if the enemy should rush headlong on you here, your Lord will help you with five thousand angels, making a tremendous onslaught" (Qur'ān, 3:125).

He has gathered rewards for those who persevere which He has not for others saying,

أُولَٰئِكَ عَلَيْهِمْ صَلَوَاتٌ مِّن رَّبِّهِمْ وَرَحْمَةٌ ۖ وَأُولَٰئِكَ هُمُ الْمُهْتَدُونَ

"They are the ones on whom God's blessings and mercy (descend), and they are the ones who receive guidance" (Qur'ān, 2:157).

Guidance, blessings, and mercy are all gathered for those who persevere and recounting all verses referring to perseverance will take quite a lengthy endeavor.

As regarding traditions, the Prophet ﷺ has said, "Perseverance is half the measure of conviction."[98]

He ﷺ has also said, "The least that you have been granted are conviction and the will to persevere: Anyone who is granted his share of them does not mind what [rewards] he has missed for not performing the night prayers or fasting during the day. If you are patient about the way you presently are, it is dearer to me than each of you bringing me a good

---

[98] *Shihab Al-Akhbar*, pp. 55, 132; Ibn Abul-Hadid, *Sharh Nahjul-Balagha*, Vol. 1, p. 319; *Al-Jami` Al-Saghir*, Vol. 2, pp. 113, 5130; *Al-Targhib wal Tarhib*, Vol. 4, pp. 5, 277; *Al-Mustadrak alal Sahihain*, Vol. 2, p. 446; *Al-Durr Al-Manthur*, Vol. 1, p. 66 and *Irshad Al-Qulub*, p. 127.

deed equal to what you all do, but I fear lest life opens up to you [with its riches and temptations] after me, so much so that each of you will not even know the other, and you will likewise be dissociated by the people of heaven at that time. One who perseveres and rests his hopes on rewards from his Lord will win the perfection of his rewards." Then he ﷺ recited this verse: "**What is with you vanishes: [whereas] what is with Allah will endure. And We will certainly bestow rewards on those who patiently persevere**" (Qur'ān, 16:96).[99]

Jabir [ibn Abdullah al-Ansari] has narrated saying that the Prophet ﷺ was asked once about conviction. He ﷺ said, "It is perseverance: One of the treasures of Paradise." He ﷺ was also asked once what conviction is. He ﷺ said, "It is perseverance."[100] This is similar to this statement of his ﷺ: "Pilgrimage is the standing at Arafa [mountain]."[101]

He ﷺ has also said, "The best of good deeds are those the souls are forced to do."[102] He ﷺ has also said, "Allah Almighty inspired to

---

[99] This is recorded by al-Faydh al-Kashani in *Al-Mahajja Al-Baydaa*, Vol. 7, p. 106.

[100] *Al-Mahajja Al-Baydaa*, Vol. 7, p. 107.

[101] See Ahmed's *Mustadrak*, Vol. 4, pp. 309-310; Ibn Majah's *Sunan*, Vol. 2, pp. 1003, 3015; al-Darmi's *Sunan*, Vol. 2, p. 59; Al-Tirmidhi's *Sunan*, Vol. 4, pp. 282, 4058; al-Nisa'i's: *Sunan*, Vol. 5, p. 256 and *Al-Mustadrak ala Al-Sahihain*, Vol. 1, p. 464.

[102] This is narrated by Sheikh Waram in *Tanbih Al-Khawatir* from Imam Ali (ع), Vol. 1, p. 63 with minor wording variation.

[Prophet] David the following: 'Adorn yourself with My norms of conduct, and among my norms of conduct is perseverance.'"[103]

Ibn Abbas, may Allah be pleased with him, has said that when the Messenger of Allah ﷺ met a gathering of the Ansar once, he said, "Are you believers (*mu'minīn*)?" They all remained silent save a man who said, "Yes, O Messenger of Allah!" The Prophet ﷺ asked, "What is the mark of your belief?" They said, "We thank the Almighty when we are prosperous and persevere when we are afflicted; we accept destiny." The Prophet ﷺ said, "Indeed you are believers, by the Lord of the Ka`ba."[104]

He ﷺ has also said, "Many rewards lie in persevering about something hated."[105]

Jesus Christ ﷺ has said, "You will not achieve what you love except through persevering about what you hate."

The Prophet ﷺ has said, "Had perseverance been a man, he would have been quite generous."[106]

He ﷺ has also said, "Islam is built on four pillars: Conviction, perseverance, *jihad* (holy war) and *adl* (Justice of God)."[107]

---

[103] *Irshad Al-Qulub*, p. 137; *Al-Mahajja Al-Baydaa*, Vol. 7, p. 207, with minor wording differences.

[104] *Al-Mahajja Al-Baydaa*, Vol. 7, p. 107. It is also narrated with some difference in wording by Muhammed ibn Humam in *Al-Tamhis*, pp. 61, 137.

[105] *Mishkat Al-Anwar*, p. 20; *Al-Mahajja Al-Baydaa*, Vol. 7, p. 107.

[106] *Tanbih Al-Khawatir*, Vol. 1, p. 40; *Al-Mahajja Al-Baydaa*, Vol. 7, p. 107.

[107] *Nahjul-Balagha*, Vol. 3, pp. 30, 157 in different wording.

He ﷺ has also said, "Perseverance's position with regard to conviction is like that of the head to the body: There can be no body for one without a head, nor can there be conviction for one who has no perseverance."[108]

Imam Ali ؑ has said, "Take to perseverance, for it is upheld by a man of determination and it is to it that a man of impatience resorts." He ؑ has also said, "If you persevere, fate will be applied to you while you receive your rewards. But if you fret, fate will apply to you while you bear your burdens."[109]

Perseverance in face of calamity and its rewards

Imam al-Hasan son of Imam Ali, peace be with them both, quotes the Messenger of Allah ﷺ saying, "There is a tree in Paradise called the Tree of Tribulation to which the people of trial and tribulation resort on the Day of Judgment where no books of reckoning will be opened about them, nor will there be scales [to weigh their deeds]; instead, rewards are poured over them." Then he ﷺ recited this verse: "**Those who patiently persevere will indeed receive a reward without measure!**" (Qur'ān, 39:10).[110]

He ؑ has also quoted the Prophet ﷺ as saying, "There is no dose dearer to Allah Almighty than one of anger which a man suppresses, or a dose of perseverance on account of a calamity. And there is no drop dearer

---

[108] *Nahjul-Balagha*, Vol. 3, pp. 82, 168; *Al-Kāfi*, Vol. 2, pp. 4, 5, 72; *Jami` Al-Akhbar*, p. 135 with minor wording difference. It is narrated in various wordings in *Al-Tamhis*, p. 64, 148 and *Mishkat Al-Anwar*, p. 21.

[109] *Nahjul-Balagha*, Vol. 3, pp. 291, 224; *Jami` Al-Akhbar*, p. 136.

[110] *Al-Durr Al-Manthur*, Vol. 5, p. 323.

to Allah Almighty than a drop of tear shed out of fear of Allah, or a drop of blood shed in the Way of Allah."[111]

He ﷺ has also been quoted as saying, "Calamities are the keys to rewards."

Imam Zainul-`Abidin ؑ has said, "When Allah ﷻ gathers the early generations and the last ones, a caller will call out: 'Where are those who persevered?! Let them enter Paradise without account.' Some people will stand up and will be received by the angels who will ask them, 'Where to, descendants of Adam?!' They will say, 'To Paradise'. The angels will ask them, 'Even before reckoning?!' They will say, 'Yes.' The angels will ask them, 'Who are you?' They will say, 'We are those who persevered.' They will ask them, 'What did you persevere about?' They will say, 'We persevered about obedience to Allah ﷻ, and we persevered about disobeying Him till Allah, the most Exalted One, the most Great, caused us to die.' The angels will then say, 'Yes, you are just as you have described. Enter Paradise. Great is the reward of those who do good.'"[112]

Anas is quoted as having said that the Messenger of Allah ﷺ has said, "Allah, the most Exalted One, the most Great, has said: *If I direct to one of My servants a calamity from Me in his body, wealth or children, and if he*

---

[111] *Ibid.*, Vol. 2, p. 74.

[112] *Kashf Al-Ghumma*, Vol. 2, p. 103 with minor wording difference. It is also narrated in different wording in Al-Tusi's *Amali*, Vol. 1, p. 100, in *Fiqh Al-Ridha*, p. 268 and in *Tanbih Al-Khawatir*, Vol. 2, p. 180.

receives all of this with beautiful perseverance, I will be too shy on the Judgment Day to set up scales for him or open records (of deeds)."[113]

Ibn Mas`ūd quotes the Prophet ﷺ as having said, "If one is granted three things, it will be as though he has been granted the best of both worlds: accepting destiny, persevering about affliction and supplicating during prosperity."[114]

Ibn Abbas, may Allah be pleased with him, is quoted as having said, "I was once in the company of the Messenger of Allah ﷺ. He said [to me]: 'Young man! Shall I teach you words through which Allah will grant you benefits?' I said, 'Yes, please do so.' He ﷺ said, 'Be mindful of Allah so He may be mindful of you. Be mindful of Allah and you will [always] find Him before you. Be mindful of Allah during prosperity, He will be mindful of you during austerity. If you are in need, ask Allah. If you seek help, seek His help, and be informed that there is a great deal of goodness in what you dislike, that victory comes with perseverance, that ease follows hardship and that with every hardship there is ease.'"[115]

He ﷺ is also quoted as having said, "Torment is brought to a man in his grave. If it is brought to him from the direction of his head, it will be repelled by his recitation of the Holy Qur'ān [in this life]. If it is brought to him from the front, charity repels it. If it is brought to him from the

---

[113] *Jami` Al-Akhbar*, p. 136; *Al-Jami` Al-Saghir*, Vol. 2, pp. 242, 6043 and *Muntakhab Kanzul-`Ummal*, Vol. 1, p. 210.

[114] Al-Rawandi's *Da`awat*, pp. 121, 289; *Al-Mustatrif*, Vol. 2, p. 70 with minor wording differences.

[115] Ahmed's *Musnad*, Vol. 1, p. 307; *Al-Durr Al-Manthur*, Vol. 1, p. 66, and it is narrated with minor wording variation on p. 20 of *Mishkat Al-Anwar*.

area of his feet, his walking to the mosque repels it[116]. And perseverance shields him: It says, 'If I see something wrong, I am the one to correct it.'"

Another wording of the above is this: "If a man enters the grave, prayers stand at his right side, *zakat* (obligatory alms) on his left, kindness overshadowing him while perseverance stands nearby and says, 'Look after my fellow, for I am here for him,' meaning if they cannot repel the torment from him, he, perseverance, would do so."[117]

He ﷺ has been quoted as saying, "How amazing the matter with the *mu'min* (believer) is! His matter is all goodness, whereas this is not available for anyone else other than a believer: If he is blessed with something good, he thanks his Maker, and this will be good for him, and if he is afflicted with a calamity, he praises Allah and perseveres. So, the believer is rewarded for everything, including a morsel which he raises to his mouth." According to another narration of this tradition, the last phrase says: "... even the morsel which he raises to his wife's mouth."[118] He ﷺ has also said, "Perseverance is the best conveyance: Allah has not granted a servant of His anything better or broader than it."[119]

---

[116] *Al-Targhib wal Tarhib*, Vol. 4, p. 373.

[117] This is narrated from Abu Abdullah in *Al-Kāfi*, Vol. 2, pp. 8, 73; in *Thawab Al-A'mal*, pp. 1, 203 and in *Mishkat Al-Anwar*, p. 26 with variation in its wording.

[118] Ahmed, *Musnad*, Vol. 1, pp. 173, 177, 182; *Al-Jami` Al-Saghir*, Vol. 2, p. 148 with wording differences.

[119] Ahmed, *Musnad*, Vol. 3, p. 47; al-Tirmidhi, Vol. 3, pp. 252, 2093; *Al-Mustadrak*, Vol. 2, p. 414; and *Al-Jami` Al-Saghir*, Vol. 2, pp. 496, 7911.

The Messenger of Allah ﷺ was asked once, "Can one enter Paradise without reckoning?" He said, "Yes, everyone who is merciful, perseverant." Abu Busayr is quoted as having said, "I have heard Abu Abdullah ﷺ saying, 'A freeman is free in all his circumstances: When a calamity afflicts him, he perseveres. If tribulations pile up on him, they fail to break him down. And if he is arrested, subdued and hardship replaces his ease, he will be like the truthful and trustworthy one, Prophet Yousuf (Joseph), peace be with him: Nothing harms his freedom even if he is enslaved, confined and vanquished, and the darkness and loneliness in the well do not harm him: Allah ﷻ turned mercifully to him and made the haughty mighty one his servant after he used to be a king, so He dispatched him and was a source of mercy to a nation on his account. Such is perseverance: It is always followed with something good; so, persevere, accustom yourselves to perseverance so you may receive your rewards."[120]

Imam al-Baqir ﷺ is quoted as having said, "Paradise is surrounded with what is hated and with perseverance: So, if one perseveres about what is hated in this life, he will enter Paradise. Hell is surrounded with pleasures and desires: If one satisfies himself with its pleasures and desires, he will enter the Fire."[121]

Imam Ali ﷺ has said that the Messenger of Allah ﷺ had said, "There are three types of perseverance: during the time of a calamity, while trying to obey the Almighty, and while trying to stay away from transgression. So, if one perseveres when afflicted by a calamity till, he repels it with a good solace, Allah will record for him three hundred degrees the distance between each degree and the other is as much as

---

[120] *Al-Kāfi*, Vol. 2, pp. 6, 73; *Mishkat Al-Anwar*, p. 21.
[121] *Ibid.*, Vol. 2, pp. 7, 73.

the distance between the heavens and the earth. And if one perseveres while trying to obey [his Maker], Allah will record for him six hundred degrees, the distance between one degree and the next is like the distance between any point on earth and the [Almighty's] Arsh. If one perseveres so he may not commit a transgression, Allah will record for him nine hundred degrees, the distance between one degree and another is like that between the earth and the end of the Arsh."[122]

Perseverance upon the calamity of death

Abdullah ibn Sinan quotes Imam Abu Abdullah ﷺ saying that the Messenger of Allah ﷺ has said, "Allah, the most Exalted, the most Great, has said: *I have made the shorter life like a loan among My servants: Whoever gives Me one loan, I will grant him ten to seven hundred as much or whatever I please. And if one does not loan me, and if I take a thing from him against his will, I shall grant him three merits: If I give even a single one of them to My angels, they will be satisfied with it.*" Then Imam Abu Abdullah ﷺ went on to quote this verse of the Holy Qur'ān:

"... [Those] who, when afflicted with calamity, say: 'To Allah do we belong, and to Him do we return...;' (Qur'ān, 2:156) and this is one of the three merits. The other is this: 'They are the ones on whom God's blessings and mercy (descend)' (Qur'ān, 2:157), and the third is: 'They are the ones who receive guidance' (Qur'ān, 2:156). Then Imam Abu Abdullah ﷺ went on to say, "All this is the reward if one from whom

---

[122] *Ibid.*, Vol. 2, pp. 15, 75; *Tanbih Al-Khawatir*, Vol. 1, p. 40; *Jami` Al-Akhbar*, p. 135; *Al-Jami` Al-Saghir*, Vol. 2, pp. 114, 5137; *Muntakhab Kanzul-'Ummal*, Vol. 1, p. 208.

something is taken away [by the Almighty, such as children, wealth, etc.] against his wish."[123]

The Imam is also quoted as having said, "If one strikes on his thigh when afflicted by a calamity, he voids his rewards."[124] The greatest perseverance is one through which someone goes when afflicted the first time, and the extent of reward is measured according to the extent of the calamity; and if one renders his affairs to the Almighty after he had already been afflicted, Allah will renew the rewards for it as if he was afflicted by it that same day."

A man once asked the Prophet, "What voids rewards in a calamity?" He said, "It is when he claps his right hand on the left. Perseverance must be upheld at the time of the first shock: Whoever accepts, he will be pleased with; and whoever feels angry, on him shall the wrath [of the Almighty] descend."

Umm Salamah, wife of the Prophet, once said, "I heard the Messenger of Allah, peace and blessings of Allah be with him and his progeny, say, 'If a servant of Allah is afflicted by a calamity and he says: 'We belong to Allah, and to Him is our return; Lord! Grant me a compensation for my calamity', Allah Almighty will compensate him for his calamity and grant him better than what he had lost.'" She went on to say, "When Abu Salamah died, I said as the Messenger of Allah

---

[123] *Al-Kāfi*, Vol. 2, pp. 21, 76; *Al-Khisal*, pp. 130, 135; *Mishkat Al-Anwar*, p. 279.

[124] This is narrated almost similarly by Al-Saduq in his *Al-Faqih*, Vol. 4, pp. 298, 900.

ﷺ had commanded me; therefore, He granted me better than Abu Salamah: the Messenger of Allah ﷺ!"¹²⁵

In another rendering of this tradition, she heard the Messenger of Allah ﷺ say, "Whenever a Muslim is afflicted, he should say as he is commanded by Allah, the most Exalted, the Greatest, that is, 'We belong to Allah and to Him is our return, Lord! Grant me rewards for my calamity and give me better than it.' When Abu Salamah, may Allah be pleased with him, passed away, I (Umm Salamah) said, 'Who is a better man than Abu Salamah?! His family is the first family that migrated to the Messenger of Allah ﷺ ' then I recited the supplication at the time of affliction, and Allah granted me the Messenger of Allah, peace and blessings of Allah be with him and his progeny."

She also is quoted as having said that the Messenger of Allah ﷺ sent the son of Abu Balta`ah to ask for her hand. She goes on to say, "I said to him, 'I have a daughter, and I am a jealous woman.'" He ﷺ said, "As regarding her daughter, I supplicate to Allah to grant her independence from her, and I supplicate to Allah to take away jealousy from her."¹²⁶

In another tradition, she is quoted as having said, "Abu Salamah returned once from seeing the Messenger of Allah ﷺ and said, 'I have heard something which the Messenger of Allah ﷺ has said and which made me very happy. He ﷺ said, 'If anyone from among the Muslims is afflicted by a calamity and says, 'We belong to Allah and to Him is our return, Lord! Grant me my reward for my calamity and compensate

---

¹²⁵ Muslim, *Sahih*, Vol. 2, pp. 4, 632; *Al-Targhib wal Tarhib*, Vol. 4, pp. 2, 336 with minor wording variation.

¹²⁶ This is recorded in *Bihar Al-Anwar* and in *Al-Targhib wal Tarhib*, Vol. 4, pp. 2, 336.

me with better than what I have lost,' (اللهم آجرني في مصيبتي واخلف لي خيرا منه) Allah will do just that.'" Umm Salamah said, "I memorized this from him. When Abu Salamah passed away, I said that statement and added: 'Lord! Grant me rewards for my calamity and compensate me with better than him!' Then I pondered inwardly and said, 'How can I get anyone better than Abu Salamah?!' When my *idda* (waiting period) came to an end, the Messenger of Allah ﷺ sought permission to visit me as I was tanning a hide. I, therefore, washed my hands and granted him permission. I put down a leather pillow stuffed with palm leaves for him on which he reclined. He ﷺ sought my hand for himself, blessings and peace of Allah be with him and with his family."[127]

Ibn Abbas says that the Messenger of Allah ﷺ has said, "There is fright in death. If one of you hears about his brother having died, he must say, *'Inna Lillahi wa Inna Ilayhi Raji'oon'* (We belong to Allah, and to Him is our return), Lord! Count him among the doers of goodness; place his book of reckoning in *Illiyyīn* (the elevated) and let his progeny be good in all coming generations! Lord! And do not deprive us of its rewards, and do not try us after it.'"[128]

Imam al-Husain son of Imam Ali ibn Abu Talib, peace be upon them all, is quoted as having said that the Prophet ﷺ has said, "If one is afflicted with a calamity, and if he says *'Inna Lillahi wa Inna Ilayhi Raji'oon'*, Allah, the most Exalted and the most Great, will renew its reward for him as much as it was on the day when he was afflicted by it."[129]

---

[127] Ahmed, *Musnad*, Vol. 4, p. 27. Al-Majlisi, *Bihar Al-Anwar*, Vol. 82, p. 139.

[128] *Al-Jami' Al-Kabeer*, Vol. 1, p. 265. *Al-Futuhat Al-Rabbaniyya*, Vol. 4, p. 124. *Bihar Al-Anwar*, Vol. 82, p. 141.

[129] *Al-Jami' Al-Kabeer*, Vol. 1, p. 747. *Bihar Al-Anwar*, Vol. 82, p. 141.

Yousuf ibn Abdullah ibn Salam has said that whenever hardship hit the family of the Prophet ﷺ, he would order them to perform prayers, then he would read this verse: "Enjoin prayer on your people, and be constant in it" (Qur'ān, 20:132).

When he was traveling, Ibn Abbas received the news that his brother, Qatham, had died, so he said, *'Inna Lillahi wa Inna Ilayhi Raji'oon'*, went aside from the road, alighted from his mount, and prayed two *rak'ats* during which he prolonged the prostration. Then he walked to his she-camel as he was reciting this verse: "**Seek (God's) help with patient perseverance and prayer; it is indeed hard, except for those who are humble**" (Qur'ān, 2:45).[130]

Whenever Ibn Abbas was afflicted with a calamity, he used to perform his ablution and pray two *rak`at*, then he would say, "Lord! We have done what You commanded us; so, do perform what you promised us." Abadah ibn Muhammed ibn Abadah ibn al-Samit has said that when Abadah, may Allah be pleased with him, was passing away, he said, "Get my bed out to the courtyard. Gather my slaves, servants, neighbors and those who used to visit me." Once all these have been gathered, he said, "I see this day as the last of my life and the first night of those of the Hereafter. I do not know that perhaps I have abused you with an action or a word, and this, I swear by the One Who holds Abadah's life in His grip, means retribution on the Judgment Day. I, therefore, implore, in the Name of Allah, everyone among you whom I have harmed to seek retribution on me before my soul departs from my body."

---

[130] *Ad-Durr Al-Manthur*, Vol. 1, p. 68.

People said to Abadah, "Rather, you used to be like a father to us and a mentor, and you never committed any wrongdoing against anyone who served you." He asked them, "Have you then forgiven me?" They answered in the affirmative. He said, "Lord! Bear witness to it." Then he said, "Remember, then, my will: I implore you all not to weep; when my soul departs from my body, perform your ablution, and do it well. Then you should enter a mosque and perform prayers seeking forgiveness for Abadah and for yourselves, for Allah, the most Exalted, the most Great, has said, 'Seek (God's) help with patient perseverance and prayer'. Then you should make haste [and bury me], and do not walk behind me bearing torches and do not put underneath me any piece of colored cloth."[131]

Jabir quotes Imam al-Baqir as saying, "The extremist form of grief is wailing, slapping the face and the chest, and pulling the hair. One who wails abandons perseverance, and one who perseveres surrenders to the will of Allah and praises Allah Almighty, accepting what Allah has done; his reward will be with Allah, the most Exalted, the most Great. One who does not do so will suffer destiny as he is held in contempt, and Allah, the most Exalted and the most Great, voids his rewards."[132]

Rab`i ibn Abdullah quotes Imam al-Sādiq as saying, "Perseverance and affliction race towards the believer. He is afflicted while he perseveres. Impatience and affliction race towards the unbeliever. Affliction reaches him as he is being impatient."[133]

---

[131] Al-Majlisi, *Bihar Al-Anwar*, Vol. 82, p. 141.

[132] *Al-Kāfi*, Vol. 3, p. 222.

[133] *Ibid.*, Vol. 3, p. 223.

He ﷺ is also quoted as having cited the Messenger of Allah ﷺ as saying, "When a believer slaps his thigh at the time of grief, he voids his rewards."[134]

Mousa ibn Bakr quotes Imam al-Kaḍim ﷺ as saying, "When one beats his thigh at the time of grief, he voids his rewards."[135]

Perseverance during forms of affliction

Ishaq ibn Ammar quotes Imam al-Sādiq ﷺ as saying to him, "O Ishaq! Do not regard a calamity for which you are granted patience, and which necessitates rewards from Allah, the most Exalted One, the most Great, as a calamity. Rather, it is, indeed, a calamity when one is deprived its rewards because he did not persevere when it fell down upon him."[136]

Abu Maysarah has said, "We were in the company of Imam Abu Abdullah, peace be with him, when a man came to him and complained about a calamity that had befallen him. The Imam ﷺ said to him, 'If you persevere, you will be rewarded, and if you do not persevere, the destiny of Allah Almighty will be affected on you as you are despised.'"[137]

Imam al-Sādiq ﷺ has said, "Affliction is a decoration for the believer and a bliss for those who have reason because going through it,

---

[134] *Ibid.*, Vol. 3, p. 224.
[135] *Ibid.*, Vol. 3, p. 225.
[136] *Ibid.*, Vol. 3, p. 224.
[137] *Ibid.*, Vol. 3, p. 225.

maintaining perseverance during it, and remaining firm towards it is correction for one's degree of Iman (conviction)."[138]

The Prophet, peace and blessings of Allah be with him, has said, "We, prophets, are afflicted the most, then the believers, the best and the one lower in conviction and so on. One who tastes affliction under protection preserved for him by Allah finds it sweeter than any other bliss, and he yearns for it when he misses it because under the fires of affliction and calamity there are *anwār* (lights) of the bliss. And under the *anwār* of a bliss there are fires of affliction and trial. Many may be saved through it, and many may perish in the bliss. Allah Almighty never lauded one of His servants, starting from Adam to Muhammed, except after afflicting him then rewarding him for adoring Him as He should be adored, for the graces of Allah Almighty in reality are conclusions the beginnings of which are afflictions, and the beginnings of their conclusions are [also] afflictions. One who comes out of the net of trials and tribulations will be made a lantern for the believers, a solace for those near to Him, a guide for those who seek Him. There is nothing good in a servant who complains about a trial in the vanguard of which there are a thousand blessings followed by a thousand norms of ease. One who does not pay the dues of persevering when afflicted with a trial will be deprived of the right of thanking Him during the time of prosperity. Likewise, one who does not truly thank Him during prosperity will be deprived of the rewards of persevering during the time of affliction."[139]

---

[138] *Musbah Al-Shari'a*, p. 486.

[139] *Ibid.*, p. 487.

Prophet Job (Ayyub) ﷺ said once by way of supplicating: "Lord! You have blessed me with seventy years of prosperity, so grant me time so I may go through seventy more in trial and tribulation."[140]

Wahab has said, "Affliction for a believer is like shackles to a beast of burden and reins to camels."[141]

The Commander of the Faithful, peace be with him, has said, "The place of perseverance in conviction is like the head in the body. The head of perseverance is affliction, yet only those deeply immersed in knowledge realize it."[142]

This entire section is obtained from statements by Imam al-Sādiq, peace be with him.

Imam al-Sādiq, peace be with him, has said, "Perseverance reveals the *nūr* (light) and clarity in the believers, while impatience reveals the darkness and desolation inside them. Everyone claims to be patient, but only those who tolerate pain prove it. Everyone denies impatience, but it appears most clearly on the hypocrites because the descent of calamity and tribulation tells who is truthful and who lies. Explained, perseverance has a bitter taste; what causes upsetting is not called perseverance. Explained, impatience is the heart palpitating, the individual grieving, his color is changing, and his condition quite different. Any calamity, the beginning of which does not have tolerance for pain, surrendering and pleading to Allah Almighty, leaves one in a state of impatience, not perseverance. The beginning of perseverance is

---

[140] *Ibid.*, p. 489.

[141] *Ibid.*, p. 497.

[8] *Ibid.*, p. 497.

bitter, and its conclusion is sweet for some people. For others, it is bitter from beginning to end. One who enters through its exit enters [Paradise], whereas one who enters through its beginning exits [it]. One who knows the value of perseverance does not complain about it.[143]

Narrating the tale of Prophet Moses and al-Khidr, peace be with them both, Allah, the most Exalted and the most Great, says, "**And how can you be patient about something of which you have no knowledge?**" (Qur'ān, 18:68). One who perseveres about something which he hates and does not complain about it to others, one who does not fret when his veil is torn apart, is one about whom Allah Almighty says: "**... And convey glad tidings to those who persevere**" (Qur'ān, 2:155) which means Paradise and forgiveness. And one who welcomes calamity with open arms and perseveres quietly and with dignity is one of the elite; his lot is described by Allah Almighty thus: "**Allah is surely with those who persevere**" (Qur'ān, 2:153)."[144]

---

[143] *Musbah Al-Shari'a*, p. 498.

[144] *Ibid.*, p. 501.

Denunciation of Ancient Customs on Death of Sons and Loved Ones

Arabs during the *jahiliyya*, who had no hope for "divine rewards", nor did they fear any divine penalty, used to urge each other to persevere, for they know the value of perseverance, shaming those who would fret, preferring forbearance, adornment with clemency, seeking magnanimity and fleeing from meekness to consolation, so much so that a man who would lose his loved one, yet nobody could tell. When Islam came and spread, and when the rewards of perseverance were known and became widespread, their desire for it increased, and the status of those who were afflicted by it was elevated.

Abu al-Ahwas has said, "Ali ibn Mas`ud came to us, and he had three young sons each was as shiny as a gold dinar. We were amazed at how beautiful they looked, so he said, 'Do you envy me on their account?' We said, 'By Allah, we do. It is due to such youths that a Muslim is envied.' He, therefore, raised his head to a low ceiling where a bird had nested and laid eggs and said, 'By the one in whose hand my soul is, it is dearer to me when I shake the dust where I bury them than the nest of this bird falls and some of its eggs break,' meaning having a greater desire for reward."

Abdullah ibn Mas`ud, may Allah be pleased with him, used to teach people the Qur'ān at the mosque as he knelt down on his knees when his wife came to him with one of his sons named Muhammed. She stood at the mosque's door and signaled to him. He went out. People made room for him till the boy sat in his lap. He kept saying, "Welcome to the one who is named after someone who is much, much better than him," and he kept kissing him till he almost swallowed his saliva. Then

Abdullah ibn Mas`ud said, "By Allah! Your death and that of your brothers is less important to me than these flies." People said to him, "Do you really wish they would die?!" He said, "May Allah forgive you for questioning me! I cannot help but answering you. I desire by it goodness. As for me, I protect their interests and fear for them. Yet I heard the Messenger of Allah, peace and blessings of Allah be with him and his progeny, saying, 'Time will come to you when a man is envied for having a light burden just as he nowadays is envied for having plenty of money and sons."

Abu Dharr, may Allah be pleased with him, used to always lose his sons after their birth, so it was said to him, "You are a man for whom no sons survive." He said, "Praise is due to Allah ﷻ who takes them from the temporal abode to the eternal one."[145]

Abdullah ibn Amir al-Mazini, may Allah be pleased with him, lost to the sweeping plague seven sons on one and the same day, so he said, "I am submitting to the will of Allah as a Muslim [should]."

Abdul-Rahman ibn Othman has said, "We went to visit Mu'adh as he was sitting at the head of his son when the latter was drawing his last breaths, so we could not help weeping, and some of us sobbed. Mu'adh rebuked one who sobbed saying, "Stop it! By Allah, Allah knows that I accept it. This [situation] is dearer to me than a military campaign in which I participated in the company of the Messenger of Allah, peace and blessings of Allah be with him and with his progeny, for I heard him say, 'If one had a son, and he held him dear, and he preferred him, but when the son died and he chose to persevere in the hope for rewards,

---

[145] Al-Muttaqi al-Hindi, *Muntakhab Kanz Al-Ummal*, Vol. 1, p. 212. Al-Majlisi, *Bihar Al-Anwar*, Vol. 82, p. 142.

Allah ﷻ will replace him for the deceased one a home better than his home, and an ultimate end better than his; He will replace his affliction with rewards equal to performing the prayers, to mercy, forgiveness and pleasure from Him.'

"So, we hardly left before the boy passed away just when the caller to prayers called for the noontime prayers; therefore, we went there to pray. By the time we arrived, he had washed his son's corpse, applied *hanoot* (embalmed) and shrouded it. Someone brought a coffin for him without waiting for brothers or neighbors to cast a last look at the deceased. When we came to know about that, we rushed and said to the father, 'May Allah forgive you, O father of Abdul-Rahman! Why did you not wait for us to finish performing our prayers before being able to view our nephew?!' He said, 'We have been ordered not to let our dead wait whether they died during the night or the day.' He got down in the grave and another man got down with him. When he wanted to come out, I stretched my hand to him to pull him out of the grave, but he refused and said, 'I shall not relinquish it [your offer of assistance] due to my strength, but I hate an ignorant person may see it as a sign of my deep grief or relaxation at the time of affliction.' He then went to his meeting place and ordered some oil with which he anointed himself, some kohl with which he dyed his eyes and a garment to put on, and he on that day kept smiling more than usual, intending in its regard whatever his intention might be. Then he said, 'We belong to Allah, and to Him is our return. Allah compensates for anything [and anyone] that perishes, a consolation for every calamity, and a compensation for what one had missed.'"

It is narrated that some people were in the company of Imam Ali son of Imam al-Husayn, peace be with them both, when a servant over-grilled some meat in the open oven (*tannoor*, tandor), whereupon he rushed to it, dropping the skewers on the head of a son of Imam Ali son of Imam al-Husayn ﷺ, killing him instantly. The Imam ﷺ leaped just to see his son having already died. He turned to the servant and said, "You are free for the sake of Allah Almighty. You did not do it on purpose," then he started preparations for his son's burial.[146]

Al-Akhnaf ibn Qais is quoted as having said, "Learn clemency and perseverance, for I have done so." He was asked, "From whom did you learn?" He said, "I learned from Qais ibn Asim." He was asked, "What was the extent of his clemency?" He said, "We were sitting once in his company when his killed son was brought to him together with his tied killer, yet he did not change the way he was squatting, nor did he even interrupt what he was talking about. Then he turned to his son's killer and said, 'O son of my brother! What caused you to do what you did?' The killer said, 'I felt angry.' The father said, 'Should you insult your own self, disobey your own Lord and wipe out a number of your good deeds whenever you feel angry? Go away, for I have freed you.'"

Then al-Akhnaf ibn Qais turned to his sons and said, "Sons! Bathe and shroud your brother, and once you have done so, bring him to me so I may perform the prayers for him." When they buried their killed brother, their father said to them, "His mother is not from your tribe; she belongs to other people, and I do not think that she will be pleased with what you have done; so, pay her the blood money from my own wealth."[147]

---

[146] *Kashf Al-Ghumma*, Vol. 2, p. 81 narrated with a minor wording variation. Al-Majlisi, *Bihar Al-Anwar*, Vol. 82, p. 142.

[147] A text almost similar to this is recorded by Ibn Abd Rabbih in his book *Al-Iqd Al-Fareed*, Vol. 2, p. 136.

Al-Sadūq has narrated in his *Faqih* book that when Dharr, the son of Abu Dharr, may Allah have mercy on him, died, Abu Dharr stood at his grave, rubbed it and said, "May Allah ﷻ have mercy on you, O Dharr! By Allah! You were kind to me, and you have passed away while I am pleased with you. By Allah! Despite having lost you, no calamity has afflicted me, and I need none other than Allah ﷻ. Had it not been for the horror of the situation, I would have been pleased to be in your place. Grieving about your own condition has distracted me from grieving about that of my own. By Allah! I have not cried for you but over you; so, I wonder what has been said to you and what you have said." Then he raised his head to the sky and said, "Lord! I have forgiven him whatever he owes me of rights; so, do forgive whatever sins he has committed about You, for You are the most generous and the most kind," then he went away saying, "We have left you behind, and had we stayed with you, we would not have been able to help you at all."[148]

Al-Mibrad narrates saying that when Dharr son of Omer died, his father stood up as he was lying in state and said, "O son! We have no calamity on account of your death, and we need none except Allah ﷻ." When the son was buried, the father stood at his grave and said, "O Dharr! May Allah forgive you. We are now preoccupied with grief over you rather than with grieving about you because we do not know what you said or what was said to you [by the angels of death]. Lord! I have granted him whatever he fell short of fulfilling my rights, so do grant him whatever he has fallen short with regard to his obligations towards You and count my rewards for this supplication among his own good deeds, and increase Your favors on me, for to You do I direct my desire."

---

[148] *Uyoon Al-Kahbar*, Vol. 2, p. 313.

Omer was asked how his son had behaved with him. He said, "I never walked during the night except as he walked in front of me [to protect me at the expense of exposing himself to danger], and I never walked during the daytime except as he was behind me [out of respect for me], and he never ascended on a rooftop when I was underneath it."[149]

Some of the folks of Banu Abbas went to meet a caliph. Among them was a blind man. The caliph asked him about his blindness. The blind man said, "I spent the night once in the depth of a valley, and I did not know anyone among my Banu Abas folks who was wealthier than I was. We were hit by a torrent which wiped out my family, wealth and sons save my camel and an infant boy. The camel was unruly, and it once was frightened and fled away. I put my infant son down and ran after the camel. I did not go far before I heard my son crying, so I returned to him just to see a wolf's head started feasting on him. I was able to catch up with the camel so I would subdue it, but it gouged me with its foot on my face, smashing it, causing me to be blind. Now I have no wealth, family, son or camel."

It is narrated that Iyadh son of Uqbah al-Fahri lost a son. He got down inside his grave. A man said to him, "By Allah, he was the master of the army; so, seek Allah's recompense for such a loss." He said, "What stops me from so doing since he was yesterday my life's decoration and today, he is among my everlasting good deeds?!"

"Abu Ali" al-Razi has said, "I accompanied al-Fadhil son of Iyadh for thirty years, yet I never saw him laughing or smiling at all except on the day when his son, Ali, died. I said to him in this regard, 'Allah, Praise

---

[149] A portion of this text is cited from al-Mibrad in *Al-Kamil*, Vol. 1, p. 140.

and Exaltation belong to Him, has loved a matter to take place, so you have loved what Allah Almighty has loved."

Amr son of Ka'b al-Hindi died in Tasattur[150], so the news was kept from his father. Then the father came to know about it, but he did not express impatience but said instead, "Praise is due to Allah Who created a martyr out of my loins." Then another son was also martyred in Jurjan[151]. When news reached him about it, he said, "Praise be to Allah Who chose another martyr from my loins."

Al-Bayhaqi has narrated saying that Abdullah ibn Matraf died, so his father, Matraf, went out to meet his folks wearing very nice clothes, having anointed himself. People became angry with him and said, "Abdullah dies, yet you come out wearing nice clothes and anointed?!" He said, "Should I instead surrender, while my Lord, Praise and Exalted is He, has promised me for it three merits which are dearer to me than the world and everything in it? Allah Almighty has said, '... [Those] who say, when afflicted with calamity, 'To Allah do we belong, and to Him do we return' are the ones on whom God's blessings and mercy (descend), and they are the ones who receive guidance' (Qur'ān, 2:156-57)."

A man from Quraish invited some of his brothers for a feast. One of his sons was hit by an animal that killed him. He hid the news from his people and said to his family, "I do not want to come to know any

---

[150] Tasattur is one of the cities of Khuzestan [now southern Iran]. This word is the Arab form of Persian "Shushtar"; refer to al-Hamawi's *Mu'jam Al-Buldan*, Vol. 2, p. 29.

[151] Jurjan is a great famous city between Tabaristan and Khurasan. Refer to al-Hamawi's *Mu'jam Al-Buldan*.

woman among you who raises her voice or who cries." Then he went to his brothers. Once they have all finished eating, he started preparing to bury his son. Suddenly they saw the coffin, so they were shocked and asked about it. He provided them with the details, whereupon they were amazed about his perseverance and generosity.

It has been mentioned that a man in Yamama buried three of his sons who all were grownups, then he squatted in his place of meeting among his folks talking to them as if nothing at all had happened. He was criticized for so doing, so he said, "They were not the first to die, nor am I the only one afflicted with such a calamity. And there is no benefit in being impatient; so, why do you remonstrate with me?"

Abu al-Abbas has traced an incident to Masrooq who quotes al-Awza`i saying, "A wise man has told us saying, 'I went out seeking to guard the borders till I reached Egypt's Areesh[152] where I saw an umbrella underneath which a blind man was sitting, stretching his hands and legs as he kept saying, 'Praise belongs to You, Lord and Master! Lord! I praise You a praise which is equivalent to all the praise Your creation have praised you, like Your favor on the rest of Your creation for having preferred me exceedingly over many of those whom You have created.' I told myself that I would ask him whether he was speaking out of knowledge or is simply inspired to do so. I came close to him and greeted him. He responded to my greeting. I said to him, 'May Allah have mercy on you! I wish to ask you about something. Are you going to answer me or not?' He said, 'If I know the answer, I will inform you of it.' I said to him, 'May Allah have mercy on you! For which of His favors are you thanking Him?' He said, 'Do you not see what He has

---

[152] Areesh is a city in Egypt on the Mediterranean on the borders of Egypt with Syria; see Vol. 4, p. 113 of *Mu'jam Al-Buldan*.

done to me?' I said, 'Yes'. He said, 'By Allah, had Allah, the most Praised and the most Exalted, poured on me fire that burnt me, ordered the mountains to crush me, ordered the seas to drown me and ordered the earth to swallow me, I would not have increased in anything but love for Him, nor would have I increased but thanks to Him. I need you to do me a favor. Are you going to oblige?' I said, 'Yes, tell me what you need.' He said, 'One of my sons used to look after me during my prayer times and feed me my meals. I lost him since yesterday. Look and see if you can find him.' I said to myself that doing this man a favor would probably bring me closer to Allah, the most Exalted, the most Great. I, therefore, stood up and went looking for his son. When I was standing between sand dunes, I saw a lion that had already devoured the boy. I said to myself, 'Surely we belong to Allah, and surely to Him is our return. How shall I bring this sad news about his son to such a righteous servant of Allah?' I went to him and greeted him. He responded to my greeting. I said, 'If I ask you about something, are you going to answer me?' He said, 'If I have knowledge about it, I will tell you.' I said, 'Are you more cherished by Allah Almighty and is your status with Him closer than that of Ayyub (Job), Prophet of Allah, peace be with him?' He answered saying, 'Rather, the prophet of Allah is. He is more cherished by Allah Almighty than I am and his status with Allah Almighty is much greater than that of my own.' I said to him, 'Allah Almighty tested him, so he persevered, so much so that those who used to enjoy his company abandoned him [due to his bodily smell], and he was thrown where passersby could see him. Be informed that your son about whom you informed me and asked me to find has been ravaged by a lion; so, may Allah increase your rewards on his account.'

"The man said, 'Praise to Allah Who did not make me sigh for what this world has.' He then gasped and fell on his face to the ground. I stayed for a while with him to move him just to find out that he had already died. I said, 'Surely we belong to Allah, and to Him is surely our return. What shall I do about him? And who will help me wash his corpse, shroud, dig his grave and bury him?'

"As I was thus preoccupied, I saw riders heading to the borders, too, so I signaled to them, and they came in my direction till they faced me. They said, 'Who are you, and who is this [dead man]?' I narrated my story to them, so they tied their mounts and helped me bathe the dead man with sea water. We shrouded him with some clothes which they had with them. I advanced and offered the funeral prayers with the group. We buried him under his umbrella.

"I sat at his grave to recite the Holy Qur'ān till an hour of the night had passed. I felt drowsy, so I saw my fellow in a vision looking in the best form, wearing very beautiful outfits and sitting in a green garden wearing green outfits and reciting the Qur'ān. I said to him, 'Are you not my fellow?!' He said, 'Yes.' I said, 'What has brought you to such a status as I can see?' He said, 'Be informed that I have come in the company of those who persevere to Allah, the most Exalted, the most Great, in a degree which they did not earn except through persevering during the time of affliction and thanks in prosperity.' I then woke up."[153]

Al-Sha'bi narrated saying that he once saw a man who had just buried a son. Once he healed the dust on his grave, he said, "O son! You were a gift from the most Glorious One, the present of the One, the trust of the Able One, the flag of a Victor, then the One Who had given you has now taken you back: The One Who owns you has reclaimed you; so, Allah ﷻ has compensated me for having lost you with perseverance;

---

[153] Al-Majlisi, *Bihar Al-Anwar*, Vol. 82, p. 149.

may Allah ﷻ never deprive me of rewards on your account." Then he said, "You have nothing which you owe me, I have granted it to you, and Allah ﷻ is more Worthy of bestowing favors than I am."

When Abdul-Maliki son of Omer ibn Abdul-Aziz passed away, and so was his brother Sahl son of Omer ibn Abdul-Aziz and his slave Muzahim, all in successive days, some of their father's friends visited him to console him. Among what one man said that day to Omer was this: "By Allah! I never saw a son like yours, nor a brother like your brother, nor a slave like your slave." Omer lowered his head then said, "Repeat what you have said." The man repeated his statement, whereupon Omer ibn Abdul-Aziz said, "I swear by the One Who took them back to Him that I love nothing more than what Allah ﷻ has done."

It has also been said that when Omer ibn Abdul-Aziz was once sitting at his meeting place, his son Abdul-Malik came to him and said, "Fear Allah with regard to the oppression dealt to your brother so-and-so! By Allah! I wish the pots boiled both myself and yourself if it pleases Allah." His son went away, so his father watched him and said to himself that he would get to know his conditions. He was asked about his conditions, so Omer ibn Abdul-Aziz said, "I wish that he dies so I may claim my rewards with Allah on account of persevering in his regard."

When Abdul-Malik was sick, his father Omer ibn Abdul-Aziz visited him and asked him how he felt. He said, "I find myself in the presence of death; so, seek rewards, O father, by persevering on my account, for the rewards of Allah Almighty are much better for you than I am." His father said, "O son! Should you be in my scales [of good deeds], it is dearer to me than I should be in yours." His son said, "What you love is dearer to me than what I love." When he died, his father stood at his grave and said, "May Allah have mercy on you, O son! You were a source of pleasure at the time of your birth, you were kind at the time of growth, yet I do not wish now that you respond to me if I should call on you."

Before Abdul-Malik's death, another son of Omer ibn Abdul-Aziz died, so he sat at his head, removed the sheet from his face and kept looking at it, shedding tears. His son, Abdul-Malik, came to him and said, "O father! You should be concerned about the death that is approaching you more so than about the death that has already approached. It is as though you have rejoined your son and buried him underneath the dust with your face." Omer wept and said, "May Allah have mercy on you, O son! By Allah, your blessing has always been great since I came to know you, yet you are more useful to one whom you admonish."

Some women's perseverance as reported by scholars

It has been narrated about Anas ibn Malik saying that the son of Abu Talhah, may Allah ﷻ be pleased with him, was sick once. His father was away when the boy died. When Abu Talhah returned, he asked his wife, "What has my son done [during my absence]?" Umm Saleem, the mother of the boy, may Allah ﷻ be pleased with her, said, "He has never been so quiet." She brought him dinner, then he cohabited with her. When he was through, she said to him, "The boy has left us."

Abu Talhah went to the Messenger of Allah the next morning and told him about this incident. The Prophet ﷺ asked him, "Did you have intercourse with your wife last night?" Abu Talhah answered in the affirmative. The Prophet ﷺ said, "Lord! Bless them." A son was born to Abu Talhah.

Umm Saleem said to Abu Talhah, "Carry him [newborn] and take him to the Messenger of Allah, peace and blessings of Allah be with him and his progeny," giving him some dates. The Prophet ﷺ asked if Abu Talhah had had something with him. The latter said, "Few dates." The Prophet ﷺ took one of them, chewed it then put it in the boy's mouth, treating his palate with it and naming him "Abdullah".[154]

A man from among the Ansar said, "I saw nine of his [Abdullah's] sons each one of whom was a reciter of the Holy Qur'ān," referring to the sons of the then newborn Abdullah.[155]

---

[154] Al-Bukhari, *Sahih*, Vol. 7, p. 109. Muslim, *Sahih*, Vol. 3, p. 1689 with some minor variation in the wording. Muhammad ibn Ali al-Alawi, *Al-Ta'azi*, Vol. 25, p. 52.

[155] Al-Bukhari, *Sahih*, Vol. 2, p. 104.

According to another narrative, Abu Talhah had a son by Umm Saleem who passed away. Umm Saleem said to her family, "Do not tell Abu Talhah about his son so I may be the one to do so." She brought him dinner. He ate and drank. Then she put on more make-up than she used to. Once she saw that he was satisfied with food and had had intercourse with her, she said to him, "O Abu Talhah! Have you seen how some people lent something to a family then asked for it back, should they be prevented from having it back?" He said, "No." She said, "Then seek compensations from your Lord for your son's death." He felt angry and said to her, "You have waited till I am unclean to tell me about my son?"[156]

In another way of narrating this incident, it is said that at the end of that night, Umm Saleem said to her husband, Abu Talhah, "O father of Talhah! So-and-so folks borrowed something which they enjoyed, but when they were asked to return it, the folks found it too hard to comply." He said, "They were not fair." She then said, "Our son, who is a loan from Allah, the most Exalted One, the most Great, has been taken back by Allah," whereupon he said, *"Inna Lillahi wa Inna Alayhi Raji'oon* (We belong to Allah, and to Him is our return)". In the next morning, Abu Talhah went to see the Messenger of Allah, peace and blessing of Allah be with him and his family, whom he informed about it. The Messenger of Allah ﷺ said to him, "Allah blessed you both last night."

Umm Saleem became pregnant, and she gave birth to a son. The Messenger of Allah ﷺ rubbed his face and named him "Abdullah".

---

[156] Muslim, *Sahih*, Vol. 4, p. 1909.

In *Uyoon al-Majalis*, the incident has an interesting addition. It runs thus:

Mu'awiyah ibn Qurrah is quoted as having said that Abu Talhah used to love his son exceedingly. The son fell ill, so Umm Saleem was concerned about the effect of grief on Abu Talhah when the death of their son drew closer, so she sent him to the Messenger of Allah ﷺ. When Abu Talhah came out of his home, the son died. Umm Saleem covered her deceased son with a shirt and put him in a corner in the house, then she went to her family and said to them, "Do not tell Abu Talhah a thing."

Then she cooked some food and applied some perfume. When Abu Talhah returned from his meeting with the Messenger of Allah ﷺ, he asked about his son. She said to him, "His soul is now calm." Then he inquired whether there was food for them to eat, whereupon she brought him the food, then she offered herself to him. He had intercourse with her. When she noticed that her husband was fully composed, she said to him, "O Abu Talhah! Are you going to be angry if we return a trust which was in our custody to its people?" He said, "Praise be to Allah! Of course, I will not." She said, "Your son was a trust in our hands, and Allah Almighty has taken him back." Abu Talhah said, "I am more worthy than you of persevering."

The man stood up, took his *ghusul* [ceremonial bath] then made his ablution and offered two *rak'at salāh*. He went to the Prophet ﷺ and informed him about what they both had done. The Messenger of Allah, peace and blessings of Allah be with him and his progeny, said to him, "Allah has blessed you in your cohabitation." Then the Messenger of Allah ﷺ said, "Praise to Allah who made in my nation the likeness of the persevering woman of Banu Israel." People asked the Prophet ﷺ, "O Messenger of Allah! What was her story?"

The Prophet ﷺ said, "There was a woman in the Children of Israel who was married and had two sons. Her husband ordered her to cook food so he would invite people to partake of it, which she did. People gathered at his house, whereas the boys set out to play. They fell in a well which was inside the house. The woman hated to ruin her husband's hospitality, so she lodged them inside, pulling them by their shirts. When everything was over, her husband came in and asked her about his sons. She said, 'They are in the house.' By then she had put on some perfume, and she offered herself to her husband till he cohabited with her. He again asked where his sons were, and again she told him that they were at home. Their father called them out by their names, whereas they came out running. The woman said, 'Praise to Allah! By Allah, they were dead, but Allah Almighty brought them back to life as a reward for my perseverance.'"[157]

Something close to this is narrated in *Dalaail al-Nubuwwah* from Anas ibn Malik who has said, "We visited a man from the Ansar who was sick. We hardly left when he passed away. We put a shirt on him as his mother, an old lady, stood as his head. We said to her, 'Seek rewards from Allah Almighty for your calamity.' She asked, 'Has my son died?' We said, 'Yes.' She said, 'Is it true what you have said?' We said, 'Yes.' She stretched her hands and said, 'Lord! You know that I have surrendered my will to You and migrated to the Messenger of Allah, peace and blessings of Allah be with him and his progeny, in the hope he will help me during the times of hardship and prosperity; so, do not

---

[157] Al-Majlisi, *Bihar Al-Anwar*, Vol. 82, p. 150.

let me bear this calamity this day.' He removed the shirt from his face with his own hands, and we did not leave till we had food with him."[158]

This supplication from the woman, may Allah ﷻ have mercy on her, leads one to know Allah ﷻ and to feel comfortable with whatever He fares with those whom we love. He accepts their supplication.

One of the interesting texts which agree with the above is the *munajāt* [one's unspoken address to the Almighty] by Barkh the Black: Allah ﷻ ordered Moses, peace be with him, to whom He spoke, to ask to pray for rain for the Children of Israel after seven years of drought. Moses ﷺ went out accompanied by seventy thousand men. Allah ﷻ inspired to him thus: "How shall I respond to them while their sins have overwhelmed them? Their innermost is foul; they call on Me without truly believing in Me, and they feel safe from My Might! Go back to one of My servants called Barkh. Let him come out so I may answer his supplication."

Moses ﷺ inquired about him, but nobody seemed to know him. As Moses, peace be with him, was walking one day along a road, he saw a black slave between whose eyes there was dust marking his prostration. He was wearing a scarf which he had tied round his neck. Moses recognized him through the *nūr* which Allah Almighty had granted him, so he asked him about his name. "My name is Barkh," he said. Moses ﷺ said to him, "We have been looking for you for some time. Come out and pray for rain for us." He went out. Among what he said was this: "Lord! This is not known to be among Your actions, nor is this a sign of Your clemency; so, what has appeared to You?! Are Your

---

[158] Munqidh ibn Mahmoud al-Saqqar, *Dalaail Al-Nubuwwah*, Vol. 6, p. 50 with some wording variation. Al-Majlisi, *Bihar Al-Anwar*, Vol. 82, p. 151.

2 - Patience and its aftermath

springs now fewer in number, or has the wind rebelled, disobeying You, or has what You have with you been exhausted?! Or has Your wrath against the sinners intensified? Are You not the Forgiving One even before wrongdoers were created?! You created mercy; You commended kindness; or are You showing us that You are inaccessible, or are You concerned about the passage of time, so You speed up the penalty?!" Barkh kept supplicating till the land was flooded with rain, and the Children of Israel were wading in it.

When Barkh returned, he faced Moses, peace be with him, and asked him, "Have you seen how I argued with my Lord and how He was so fair to me?!"[159]

Now we return to reports about women who persevered:

It has been narrated that Asma daughter of Umais, may Allah be pleased with her, was informed once about the death of her son, Muhammed son of Abu Bakr, how he was killed then burnt inside a donkey's carcass. She went to her prayer area where she sat and controlled her rage till her breasts bled.

It has been narrated about Hamna daughter of Jahsh, may Allah be pleased with her, being informed about her brother having been killed. She said, "May Allah have mercy on him; we belong to Allah, and to Him do we return." Those who brought her the sad news added saying, "Your husband, too, has been killed." She said, "How grieved I am!" The Messenger of Allah, peace and blessings of Allah be with him and

---

[159] Al-Dumairi has detailed this incident in his book *Hayat Al-Haywan Al-Kubra*, Vol. 1, p. 247.

his progeny, therefore said, "A husband has a branch from the wife which is not like anything else."[160]

It has also been reported that Safiyya daughter of Abdul-Muttalib went to see her brother by both her parents, Hamzah son of Abdul-Muttalib, at Uhud, and his corpse had been mutilated. The Prophet, peace and blessings of Allah be with him and his progeny, told her son, al-Zubair, to send her back so she would not see in what condition her brother was. Al-Zubair said to her, "Mother! The Messenger of Allah, peace and blessings of Allah be with him and his progeny, orders you to return." She said, "Why so, since I have already been told that my brother's corpse has been mutilated? This is decreed by Allah, the most Exalted, the most Great; so, why should we object to His will? I shall seek His rewards for it, and if Allah wills, I shall persevere." When al-Zubair went to the Prophet, peace and blessings of Allah be with him and his progeny, he told him about what she said. He, therefore, told al-Zubair not to stand in her way. She came and cast a look at the corpse, offered prayers and said, "We belong to Allah and to Him is our return," then she prayed the Almighty to forgive him.[161]

Ibn Abbas, may Allah be pleased with him, is quoted as having said that when Hamzah, may Allah be pleased with him, was killed during the Battle of Uhud, Safiyya [his sister] came looking for him, not knowing what had happened to him. She met Ali ﷺ and al-Zubair. Ali, peace be with him, said to al-Zubair, "Say something to your mother." Al-Zubair said, "No, you say something to your aunt." She said, "How did Hamzah fare?" They gave her the impression that they did not know.

---

[160] Ibn Majah, *Sunan*, Vol. 1, p. 507; *Al-Mustadrak ala Al-Sahihain*, Vol. 4, p. 62.

[161] Ibn Hisham, *Seera*, Vol. 3, p. 103.

She went to the Prophet, peace and blessings of Allah be with him and his progeny, whereupon he ﷺ said that he was afraid she, his aunt, might lose her sanity. He ﷺ, therefore, put his hand on her chest and supplicated for her. She said, "We belong to Allah, and to Him is our return," and she wept. The Prophet, peace and blessings of Allah be with him and his progeny, stood up and saw how mutilated his uncle's corpse was. He ﷺ said, "Had I not been concerned about women losing their patience, I would have left him till he is gathered on the Judgment Day from birds' craws and beasts' bellies."[162]

A youth from among the Ansar named Khallad was martyred during the Battle of Banu Quraizah. His mother came neatly outfitted. It was said to her, "Do you dress yourself like that while you have been afflicted with Khallad?!" She said, "If I have been afflicted with Khallad, I am not afflicted with my modesty." The Prophet ﷺ supplicated for him, saying, "He will receive twice the rewards because the People of the Book [the Jews of Banu Quraizah] had killed him."[163]

Anas ibn Malik is quoted as having said that during the Battle of Uhud, the people of Medina were extremely agitated. They said, "Muhammed, peace and blessings of Allah be with him and his progeny, has been killed," so much so that loud cries were heard in all city districts. A woman from the Ansar came out grieving. She saw the corpses of her father, son, husband, and brother; nobody knows which one of them she first saw. When she saw the last corpse, [not recognizing any of them] she asked: "Who is this?" She was told, "This is your brother, and these are your father, husband and son." She said, "How did the

---

[162] *Al-Mustadrak ala Al-Sahihain*, Vol. 3, p. 197.

[163] *Muntakhab Kanzul-Ummal*, Vol. 1, p. 212 with some variation in its wording.

Prophet, peace and blessings of Allah be with him and his progeny, fare?" They said, "He is ahead of you." She walked till she met the Prophet ﷺ. She held a portion of his robe and kept saying, "O Messenger of Allah! May both my parents be sacrificed for your sake! I do not care about anything as long as you are safe from any harm."

Al-Bayhaqi has narrated saying that the Messenger of Allah, peace and blessings of Allah be with him and his progeny, met once a woman from Banu Dinar whose husband, father and brother were killed defending the Prophet, peace and blessings of Allah be with him and his progeny, during the Battle of Uhud. When she received condolences because of them, she asked, "How did the Messenger of Allah, peace and blessings of Allah be with him and his progeny, fare?" They said, "He fared well, O mother of so-and-so, and he praises Allah as you love." She said, let me see him." They pointed in his direction. When she saw him, she said, "Any calamity, other than one harming you, is nothing at all."[164]

Samra daughter of Qais, sister of Abu Hizam, came out when both her sons were killed. The Prophet, peace and blessings of Allah be with him and his progeny, consoled her in their regard, so she said to him, "Any calamity other than one afflicting you is nothing. By Allah! This dust which I see on your face is more painful to me than seeing what has taken place to them."

It has been narrated that Silah son of Asheem was participating in a military campaign accompanied by his son. He said to his son, "O son! Charge and fight, so I may seek Allah's rewards." The son charged, fought, and was killed. His father then charged, fought, and was killed,

---

[164] Ibn Hisham, *Seera*, Vol. 3, p. 105. This is also narrated by Al-Waqidi in his *Maghazi*, Vol. 1, p. 292 with some difference in wording.

too. Women gathered round his mother, Mu'adha al-Adawiyya wife of Silah. She said to them, "Welcome to you if you have come to congratulate me [on my son's martyrdom]. But if you have come for another reason, go back."

It has been narrated that an old woman from Banu Bakr son of Kilab used to be praised by her folk for her wisdom and terse opinions. One of those who were in her company once was told that her son, the only son she had had, died following a long period of sickness during which she nursed him very well. When he died, she sat in her courtyard where her folk came to offer their condolences. She asked one of their dignitaries: "O so-and-so! What is the duty of one on whom a blessing has been poured, one who has been outfitted with good health, one whose vision is straight…, should he not be self-confident before his knot is untied and he sits in his courtyard, death descending upon his house, so he can keep it [death] away from himself?" She then recited a couple of lines of poetry saying,

He is my son, my joy, and the Lord of Dignity has taken him to Himself,
So, if I rest my hope on rewards, and if I grieve, what benefit will tears bring me?

A dignitary said to her, "We always hear that women are too weak to persevere; so, nobody after you should ever fret. Your perseverance is honored, and surely you are not at all like other women." She said to him, "If one differentiates between fretting and persevering, he will find between them a huge distance: As for perseverance, it looks good in the open, it is well rewarded. As for fretting, it does not bring about anything good while causing one who goes through it to reap a sin. Had they both had forms of two men, perseverance would have been the winner, and it will have the good image, the honorable nature with regard to the creed and the good rewards in the Hereafter. Suffices him what Allah, the most Exalted One, the most Great, has promised those in whom He instills it."

Juwairiyya daughter of Asma is quoted as having said that three brothers participated in the Battle of Tasattur and were all martyred. Their mother heard about their martyrdom, so she asked, "Were they killed charging, or were they fleeing?" It was said to her that they were charging. She said, "Praise be to Allah! By Allah! They have won, and they have safeguarded their honor! I wish I could sacrifice both my parents for their sake!" She neither sighed, nor did she shed one tear.

Abu Qudamah al-Shami (the Syrian) is quoted as having said, "I was in command of the army in an invasion. I entered a country and called people to participate in the campaign, trying to make them interested in and recruit them for Jihad, mentioning the distinction of martyrdom and the rewards of the martyrs. Then people dispersed, so I rode my horse and went home. I met a woman whose face was the very best, and she called on me by my name, but I kept going and did not respond. She said, 'Such is not the attribute of the righteous.' I, therefore, stopped. She came and gave me a sheet of paper wrapped in a piece of cloth then went back in tears. I looked at the sheet and I found this written in it: 'You invited us to participate in Jihad and made us desire its rewards. I cannot do that [being a woman], so I cut off the best in me: both my braids and sent them to you to put them in your horse's reign, perhaps Allah will see my hair tied to your horse and He may forgive me.' When the morning of fighting approached, I saw a youth fighting between the ranks with his head uncovered. I advanced towards him and said, 'Young man! You are a praiseworthy youth, and you are on your feet; I see no security for you if the steeds charge and they may crush you under their hooves; so, go back from your position.' The youth said, 'Do you order me to return while Allah Almighty has said: **O you who believe! When you meet the unbelievers in hostile array, never turn your backs to them (Qur'ān, 8:15)?'** He completed the recitation of the verse up to its end. I, therefore, made him ride on a camel which was with me. He said, 'O Abu Qudamah! Loan me three arrows.' I said, 'Is this the time for a loan?!' He kept insisting till I said to him, 'I shall do so on one condition: If Allah grants you martyrdom, include me in your intercession.' He said, 'Yes, I shall do that.' So, I gave him three arrows. He put one arrow in his bow and shot it, killing one Roman. Then he shot another and killed another Roman. Then he shot the remaining third arrow as he said, 'Peace be with you, O Abu Qudamah, a greeting of someone bidding you farewell.' An arrow came to him, piercing his face between his eyes. He put his head on the saddlebow. I advanced towards him and said, 'Do not forget it [your promise].' He said, 'Yes, I will not, but I need a favor of you: When you enter Medina, go to my mother and hand over my saddlebag to her and inform her, for she is the one who had given you her hair so you would tie it to your horse. Greet her, for last year, she lost my father, and this year she has lost me.' He then died, so I dug up a grave for him and buried him. When I was about to leave his grave behind, the earth threw his corpse out on the ground. Some people said, 'He is a praiseworthy youth, and maybe he went out [for Jihad] without his mother's permission.' I said, 'The earth accepts one who is more evil [than one who goes to Jihad without first getting his parents' permission due to his age].' I stood up and prayed two *rak'at*, supplicating to the Almighty, whereupon I heard a voice saying, 'O Abu Qudamah! Leave the servant of Allah alone!' Soon, birds [scavengers] descended on his corpse and ate it.

"When I returned to Medina, I went to his mother's house. Having knocked at the door, his sister came out to me. When she saw me, she [immediately] returned to her mother and said, 'Mother! This is Abu Qudamah, and my brother is not with him. We were afflicted last year with the loss of my father and this year with the loss of my brother.' His mother came out and asked me, 'Have you come to offer condolences or congratulations?' I said, 'What do you mean?' She said, 'If my son passed away, console me. But if he won martyrdom, congratulate me.' I said, 'No, he has died as a martyr.' She said, 'His death has a mark; have you seen it?' I said, 'Yes, I have: The earth did not accept him, and birds descended and ate his flesh, leaving his bones which I buried.' She said, 'Then praise be to Allah!' I handed the saddlebag to her. She opened it and took out a shirt from it and iron chains. She said, 'Whenever night overwhelmed him with its darkness, he would wear this shirt and tie himself with the chains. He would thus speak to his Creator saying: Lord! Resurrect me from the claws of birds! Allah, praise and to Him, responded to his supplication, may Allah have mercy on him.'"

Al-Bayhaqi quotes Abu Abbas al-Sarraj as saying, "Someone lost a son, so I went to see his mother to whom I said, 'Fear Allah and be patient.' She said, 'My calamity of losing him is greater than I should ruin it with impatience.'"

Aban ibn Taghlib, may Allah have mercy on him, has said, "I visited a woman whose son had just died. She came out to him, closed his eyelids, and directed his corpse towards the Ka'ba. Then she said, 'O son! What good is fretting about something which never lasts? Weeping should be over what will tomorrow descend on you. O son! Taste what your father tasted, and after you your mother shall taste it, too. The greatest rest for this body is sleep, and sleep is a sibling of death. What difference should it make to you whether you sleep on your bed or on something else? Tomorrow there will be questioning, Paradise and Hell; if you are among the residents of Paradise, how can death bring you any harm at all? And if you are among the residents of Hell, what benefit should life bring you even if you live longer than anyone else? By Allah, O son, had death been among the most of noble things for the descendants of Adam, Allah would not have caused His Prophet, peace and blessings be with him and his family, to die while keeping His enemy, Satan the accursed, alive.'"[165]

[Abul-Abbas Muhammed ibn Yazid] al-Mubarrad is quoted as having said, "I went to a woman to offer condolences on the death of her son. She kept praising him saying, 'He, by Allah, toiled but not for his own belly and commanded but not his wife. He was a hard worker for any cause which would not bring him shame. If there is a sin, he would not tolerate it.' I said to her, 'Do you have a son by him?' She said, 'Yes, praise to Allah; one with a lot of goodness, a reward from Allah Almighty and a good compensation in this life and in the life to come.'"

He also is quoted as having said that he went once to Yemen and stayed at the residence of a woman who had a lot of money, slaves, sons, and prosperity. He stayed there for a while. When he wanted to depart, he asked her, "Is there anything I can do for you?" She said, "Yes. Whenever you come to this land, stay with us." He stayed away for years, then he returned and stayed at her residence but found out that her wealth and slaves had gone, her sons had died, and her home was sold, yet she was pleased and smiling. He said to her, "Do you smile despite all what has befallen you?" She said, "O servant of Allah! When I was in prosperity, I had a lot of grief, so I knew that it was because I did not thank the Almighty enough for it. Now I am in this condition, I smile and thank Allah Almighty for the patience which He has granted me."

---

[165] Al-Majlisi, *Bihar Al-Anwar*, Vol. 82, p. 152.

Muslim ibn Yasar has said once, "I went to Bahrain where a women hosted me, and she had sons, slaves, wealth and prosperity, yet I always saw her sad. I stayed away from her for a long period of time then I returned. I did not find anyone at her door, so I sought permission to enter, and I found her pleased and smiling. I said to her, 'How are you?' She said, 'During the time when you were away from us, every time we sent something by the sea, it sank, nor anything by land except it defected. The slaves are gone, the sons are dead.' I said to her, 'May Allah have mercy on you! I found you looking sad during that time and now you are pleased!' She said, 'Yes, when I was at ease, I was afraid Allah Almighty might have sped up the rewards for my good deeds in the short life. When my wealth, sons and slaves were gone, I hoped that Allah Almighty might have saved something for me with Him.'"[166]

Someone has said, "I went out with a friend to the desert where we were lost. We saw a tent on the right side of the road, so we went to it and pronounced the greeting. A woman responded to our greeting and asked us who we were. We said, 'We have lost our way, so we came to you, feeling comfortable with you.' She said, 'Men! Get your faces away from me till I do what you deserve.' We did. She threw a shirt to us and said, 'Sit on it till my son returns.' Then she kept raising a portion of the tent then putting it down till she raised it once and said, 'I ask Allah for the blessing of what is approaching. The camel belongs to my son, but the rider is not he.' The rider addressed the woman saying, 'O mother of Aqeel! May Allah greatly reward you because of your son, Aqeel.' She said, 'Woe on you! Has he died?' He said, 'Yes.' She said, 'What was the cause of his death?' He said, 'Camels crowded around him and threw him into a well.' She said to him, 'Alight and perform the duty for these folks,' pushing a ram to him which he slaughtered

---

[166] *Ibid.*, Vol. 82, p. 152.

and cooked. He presented food to us. We kept eating and wondering about how patient she was.

"Having finished eating, she came out to us and said, 'O folks! Is there among you one who is good at reciting something from the Book of Allah?' I said, 'Yes.' She said, 'Then recite for me verses in which I find solace for the loss of my son.' I told her that Allah Almighty says: **Convey glad tidings to those who patiently persevere, those who, when afflicted with calamity, say: To Allah do we belong, and to Him is our return. They are the ones on whom Allah's blessings and mercy (descend), and they are the ones who receive guidance (Qur'ān, 2:155-57).**' She said, 'By Allah tell me, are these written like that in the Book of Allah?' I said, 'By Allah they are as such in the Book of Allah.' She said, '*Assalamu Alaykum.*' She stood and offered *rak'at* then said, 'Lord! I have done what You have ordered me, so fulfill what You have promised me. Had one stayed for one—it is there that I said to myself: She would say: My son would have stayed for me due to my need for him—Muhammad, peace and blessings of Allah be with him and his progeny, would have stayed for his nation.'

"I came out saying this to myself: 'I have never seen a more perfect woman like her or more generous. She mentioned her Lord in the most perfect of His attributes and the most beautiful. Finding death unavoidable, and that fretting is futile, that weeping does not bring back a mortal, she returned to good patience, resting her hope on rewards with Allah Almighty as a treasure for the Day of want and need.'"[167]

About the same has been narrated by Ibn Abul-Dunya who has said, "A man used to keep me company, then I heard that he was sick. I went to visit him, and I found him about to die. His mother, an old woman,

---

[167] *Ibid.*, Vol. 82, p. 152.

was with him. She kept looking till his eyelids were closed, his head bandaged, and his corpse was directed towards the Ka'ba. Then she said, 'May Allah have mercy on you, O son! You were kind to us, affectionate, and now Allah has granted me patience in your regard. You used to stand for long praying, you used to fast quite often; may Allah Almighty not deprive you of the mercy I hope He will show you, and may He grant us good solace.' Then she looked at me and said, 'O visitor of the sick! You have seen a preacher, and so have we.'"

I persevered, and perseverance always rewards well,
Is impatience beneficial so I may lose my patience?
I persevered about that if a little of it is borne by
Mountains in Radwa, they would have cracked.
I suppressed my tears then sent them back,
Now the heart, not the eyes, is tearful.

"I said, 'O woman, what have you been so patient about?' She said, "A calamity that befell me which never afflicted anyone else at all.' I asked her, 'What was it?' She said, 'I used to have two lion cubs [sons] playing before my eyes. Their father sacrificed two sheep for Eid al-Adha. One of them said to his brother, 'O brother! Let me show you how our father sacrificed his sheep.' He stood up, took a knife, and slaughtered his brother. The killer ran away. Their father entered. I said, 'Your son has killed his brother then fled away.' He went out looking for him, then he found out that a lion had devoured him. The father returned but died on the way back out of thirst and hunger.'"

Someone else narrated this same incident, adding that he saw a beautiful woman showing no signs of grief. She said, "By Allah! I know nobody who has been afflicted as I have been," and narrated the incident. He said to her, "How do you fare with impatience?" She said, "Had I found it helpful, I would not have preferred anything else over it, and had it lasted for me, I would have lasted for it."

Someone has said that a woman was afflicted by the death of her son, and she persevered. She was asked about it, so she said, "I have preferred to obey Allah Almighty over obedience to Satan."

3 - Acceptance

Allah Almighty has said,

$$\text{لِكَيْلَا تَأْسَوْا عَلَىٰ مَا فَاتَكُمْ وَلَا تَفْرَحُوا بِمَا آتَاكُمْ}$$

"... So that you may not despair over matters that pass by, nor exult over favors bestowed upon you" (Qur'ān, 57:23).

$$\text{رَضِيَ اللَّهُ عَنْهُمْ وَرَضُوا عَنْهُ}$$

"Allah is pleased with them and they with Him" (Qur'ān, 5:119; 9:100; 58:22 and 98:8).

Be informed that acceptance [of whatever Allah ﷻ decrees] is the fruit of love for Allah ﷻ: One who loves something does it, and love is the fruit of knowledge. When one loves an individual because he has some attributes of perfection or qualities of beauty, this love increases whenever he gets to know him more and more and thinks about him.

If one ponders on the greatness and perfection of Allah Almighty, the explaining of some of which is quite lengthy and gets us out of the gist of this message, he would love Him, and the believers love Allah ﷻ the most. When one loves Him, he sees as good anything that He does, and this is called acceptance.

Acceptance, then, is the fruit of love. Actually, it is the fruit of every type of perfection. Since it is a branch of knowledge, one who ponders on His mercy would plead to Him [for it]. One who ponders on His greatness fears Him. When one cannot reach the one whom he loves, he yearns for him. And when he reaches him, he feels comfortable with him. When there is extreme comfort of this sort, it produces joy. When one sees how He cares [about everyone and everything], he would rely on Him. And when one sees as good whatever He does, he becomes pleased with Him. As he sees how faulty he is compared to His perfection, His full knowledge of and control over the one whom He loves, he surrenders to Him. From such surrender great stations branch out; some of those who know them know them, and these reach the ultimate end of every type of perfection.

Be informed that acceptance is a great virtue for man. Actually, all virtues are rendered to it. Allah Almighty has drawn attention to its distinction, making it conjoint with the acceptance of Allah Almighty and a mark pointing to it:

رَضِيَ اللَّهُ عَنْهُمْ وَرَضُوا عَنْهُ

"Allah is pleased with them and they with Him" (Qur'ān, 5:119).

But the greatest bliss is the good pleasure of Allah ﷻ: that is the supreme joy; such is the ultimate end of benevolence, the zenith of gratitude.

The Prophet, peace and blessings of Allah be with him and his progeny, has made it a guide to conviction (*imān*). When he asked a group from among his companions: "Who are you?" They said, "Believers." He asked them, "What is the mark of your belief?" They said, "We persevere when afflicted, we thank when prosperous and we accept when destiny befalls." He said, "Believers, you are, by the Lord of the Ka'ba."[168]

He, peace, and blessings of Allah be with him and his progeny, also said, "If Allah loves one of His servants, He tries him with affliction: If he perseveres, He will choose him; when he is pleased, He will count him among the elite ones."[169]

He, peace and blessings of Allah be with him and his progeny, has also said, "When it is Judgment Day, Allah Almighty will plant wings for a group from among my nation whereby they will fly from their graves to Paradise where they roam about and enjoy as they please. The angels will ask them, 'Did you witness the Reckoning?' They would say, 'We did not witness any Reckoning.' They would ask them, 'Did you pass on the Sirat?' They would say, 'We saw no Sirat.' They would ask them, 'Did you see Hell?' They would say, 'We did not see any such thing.' The angels would then say, 'To which nation do you belong?' They would answer saying, 'We belong to the nation of Muhammad, peace and blessings of Allah be with him and his progeny.' The angels would then ask them, 'We plead to you in the Name of Allah to tell us how your deeds in life were.' They would say, 'There were two attributes in them. It is through them that Allah Almighty got us to reach this status

---

[168] This is narrated in some difference in wording in *Al-Tamhees*, Vol. 61, p. 137; *Da'aim Al-Islam*, Vol. 1, p. 223; and it is cited by al-Faydh al-Kashani in his work *Al-Mahajja Al-Baydaa*, Vol. 7, p. 107.

[169] *Al-Mahajja Al-Baydaa*, Vol. 8, pp. 67, 88. *Bihar Al-Anwar*, Vol. 82, pp. 26, 142.

through the favor of His mercy.' The angels would ask them about these two attributes, and they would answer saying, 'Whenever we were by ourselves, we felt too shy to be disobedient of Allah; and we were always pleased with whatever He allotted for us.' The angels will say, 'What you now have rightfully belongs to you.'"[170]

He, peace, and blessings of Allah be with him and his progeny, has also said, "Grant Allah ﷻ acceptance from your hearts, you will thus win the rewards of Allah Almighty on the Day of your want and bankruptcy."[171]

In narratives about Moses, peace be with him, he was asked once: "Ask your Lord about something because of which, if we do it, He would be pleased with us." Allah Almighty inspired to him saying, "Tell them to be pleased with Me so I may be pleased with them."[172]

Similar to the above is narrated about our Prophet, peace and blessings of Allah be with him and his progeny, who has said, "If one likes to know what is there for him with Allah, the most Exalted One and the most Great, let him look and see what status he has for Allah with him, for Allah Almighty grants one the status which he himself grants Allah."

In a narrative about David, peace be with him, the Almighty says this to him: "Why should My friends be concerned about this life? Concerns

---

[170] *Al-Mahajja Al-Baydaa*, Vol. 8, p. 88.

[171] Al-Kolayni has narrated something similar to this text in Vol. 2, pp. 141, 203 of his book *Al-Kāfi*. Al-Majlisi cites it in Vol. 82, p. 143 of *Bihar Al-Anwar*.

[172] *Al-Mahajja Al-Baydaa*, Vol. 8, p. 88; *Bihar Al-Anwar*, Vol. 82, p. 143.

remove the sweetness of their addressing Me with their hearts. O David! I love My friends to be spiritual, worry-free."[173]

It has been narrated that Moses, peace be with him, has said, "Lord! Guide me to something I should do which causes You to be pleased with me so I may do it." Allah Almighty inspired him saying: "My pleasure lies in something which you dislike, and you cannot persevere about something which you dislike." He said, "Lord! Lead me to it! Lord! Lead me to it!" The Almighty said, "My pleasure is in your acceptance of My judgment."[174]

Prophet Moses, peace be with him, asked Allah: "Oh Lord who is the most beloved to you amongst your slaves?" Allah answered, "the one who when I take his beloved makes peace with me." Moses then asked: "who amongst your slaves are you angry with." Allah answered, "he who consults with me but when I set the course of matters is unpleased with the outcome."

Something more emphatic has been narrated than the above, that is, the Almighty has said, "It is I, Allah; there is no god but I; one who is not patient when I afflict him, and he does not accept my judgment, should seek a god other than I."[175]

It has also been narrated that Allah Almighty inspired this to David, peace be with him: "O David! You want something, whereas I want something else. What shall be is what I want. If you surrender to what

---

[173] Al-Majlisi, *Bihar Al-Anwar*, Vol. 82, p. 143.

[174] Al-Rawandi, *Da'awat*, p. 71. *Bihar Al-Anwar*, Vol. 82, p. 143.

[175] Al-Rawandi, *Da'awat*, p. 74. *Al-Jami' Al-Saghir*, Vol. 2, pp. 235, 6010 with a wording variation.

I want, I shall spare you what you want. But if you do not surrender to what I want, I will wear you out regarding what you want, and [in the end] only what I want shall come to be."[176]

Ibn Abbas has been quoted as saying, "The first to be called on to enter Paradise on the Judgment Day will be those who praise Allah Almighty under any condition."[177]

Ibn Mas'ud is quoted as having said, "Should I lick a piece of burning timber, and it burns whatever it burns, keeping whatever it keeps, it is dearer to me than I say about something which happened that I wished it did not, or about something which did not happen that I wished it did."

The Prophet, peace and blessings be with him and his progeny, is quoted as having said, "Allah Almighty, through His wisdom and greatness placed spirituality and ease in acceptance [of Allah's decrees] and in conviction, and He made grief and sadness in doubt and rage."[178]

[Imam] Ali son of [Imam] al-Husayn, peace be with them both, has said, "Asceticism is [divided into] ten portions: The highest degree of asceticism is the lowest degree of piety. The highest degree of piety is the lowest degree of conviction. And the highest degree of conviction is the lowest degree of acceptance [of Allah's decrees]."[179]

---

[176] *Al-Tawhid*, pp. 4, 337.

[177] Al-Majlisi, *Bihar Al-Anwar*, Vol. 82, p. 143.

[178] *Al-Mahasin*, pp. 17, 47; *Mishkat Al-Anwar*, pp. 12, 13; *Al-Jami' Al-Saghir*, Vol. 1, pp. 382, 2493; *Muntakhab Kanzul-Ummal*, Vol. 1, pp. 178, 256, 257.

[179] *Al-Kāfi*, Vol. 2, pp. 6, 50.

3 - Acceptance

[Imam] al-Sādiq, peace be with him, has said, "The attribute of acceptance is that you accept what you like and what you do not like. Acceptance is a ray of the light of Gnosticism. One who accepts forgets about all his choices. One who truly accepts is one who is truly accepted, and acceptance combines in it the meaning of adoration. The meaning of acceptance is the pleasure of the hearts. I have heard my father, Abu Muhammed al-Baqir, peace be with him, say, 'One whose heart is attached to an existent is a *mushrik* [committing *shirk*, apostasy]. One whose heart is attached to something which he will [eventually] lose commits *kufr* [disbelief]. Both such persons are outside the norm of acceptance. And I wonder about one who claims to worship Allah while disputing with Him about whatever He decrees! Accepting Gnostics are far from it.'"

It has been narrated that Jabir ibn Abdullah al-Ansari, Allah be pleased with him, was afflicted in his last days with weakness, old age, and incapacitation [blindness]. He was visited by [Imam] Muhammed ibn Ali al-Baqir, peace be with him, who asked him about his condition. He said, "I am in a status in which I prefer old age over youth, sickness over health and death over life." Al-Baqir, peace be with him, said, "As for me, O Jabir, if Allah causes me to age, I shall love old age, if He keeps me young, I shall love young age. If He causes me to fall sick, I shall love sickness. If he heals me, I shall love healing and good health. If He causes me to die, I shall love death, and if He decrees to keep me alive, I shall love to stay alive." When Jabir heard the Imam say so, he kissed his face and said, "Surely the Messenger of Allah, peace and blessings of Allah be with him and his progeny, told the truth when he said, 'You shall live long enough to meet one of my sons whose name is the same as mine, who prowls knowledge like an ox ploughs the land," so he was called "Baqir", one who prowls the knowledge of the early generations and of the last, that is, he splits it open and gets to the pith, the heart, the essence of it.

It has been narrated that al-Kolayni, through his *isnad* (reference) to Abu Abdullah, peace be with him, says, "The head of obedience to Allah is patience and acceptance of whatever comes from Allah, be it something one loves or hates, and whenever a servant of Allah is pleased with Him regarding anything which he loves or hates, he will have goodness in whatever he loves or hates."[180]

Through his *isnad* back to this same Imam, peace be with him, the latter says, "One who knows Allah Almighty the most; is one who is the most pleased with whatever Allah, the most Exalted One, the most Great, decrees."[181]

Through his *isnad* also to the Imam ﷺ, the latter says, "Allah Almighty has told his Prophet: 'I do not turn My believing servant from something except that I decree goodness in it for him; so, let him accept My decree, let him be patient about My affliction, and let him thank My blessings, for I shall write him, O Muhammed, in the company of the Truthful Ones with Me.'"[182]

He, peace be with him, has said, "Among what Allah, the most Exalted One and the most Great, inspired to Moses, peace be with him, was this: 'O Moses son of Imran [Amram]! I have not created anything dearer to Me than a believing servant: When I afflict him [with a trial], I do so for his own good. When I grant him health, it is for his own

---

[180] *Al-Kāfi*, Vol. 2, pp. 1, 49.
[181] *Ibid.*, Vol. 2, pp. 2, 49.
[182] *Ibid.*, Vol. 2, pp. 6, 50.

goodness. When I keep away something from him, it is for his own good, and I know best what My servant needs for his own good; so, let him persevere when I afflict him, let him appreciate My blessings, and let him accept my judgment, for I shall then write him down among the Truthful Ones with me if he does what pleases Me and obeys My command.'"[183]

It has been said this to [Imam] al-Sādiq, peace be with him: "Through what criterion a believer is identified as such?" He said, "It is through full surrender to Allah and acceptance of whatever He decrees on him, be it something with which he is pleased or displeased."[184]

It has been narrated in books of the Israelites that a servant worshipped Allah Almighty for a very long period of time, so he saw in a vision that his so-and-so female companion was in Paradise. He asked about her and hosted her for three days and nights in order to observe how she behaved. He used to stand for prayers during the night as she remained asleep. He kept fasting as she was not. He, therefore, said to her, "Have you done anything else other than what I have observed?" She said, "By Allah, I have not done anything other than what you have seen, and I am not familiar with anything else." He kept insisting on her to remember something till she said, "I remember only one single attribute: Whenever I was in hardship, I did not wish to be in prosperity; whenever I was sick, I did not wish to be healthy, and whenever I was under the sun, I did not wish to be in the shade." The worshipper put his hands on his head and said to her: "Is this just an

---

[183] *Al-Kāfi*, Vol. 2, pp. 7, 51. Al-Mufid, *Aamali*, Vol. 2, p. 93. Al-Tusi, *Aamali*, Vol. 1, p. 243. *Al-Mu'min*, Vol. 9, p. 17. *Al-Tamhees*, pp. 55, 108. *Mishkat Al-Anwar*, p. 299.

[184] *Al-Kāfi*, Vol. 2, pp. 12, 52.

attribute?! This, by Allah, is a great attribute which an adoring servant of Allah finds to be very difficult to achieve."

Acceptance- A Golden path

The station of acceptance is much higher than that of patience. Rather, the ratio of patience compared to acceptance among the people who know the truth is the same as disobedience compared to obedience: Love requires finding pleasure in affliction because one yearns for the company of the one whom he loves much more when he is afflicted than when he is not; so, he desires his presence and company. Patience requires hating affliction and finding it hard till patience forces one to accept it. Hating something is the opposite of feeling at ease with it; thus, patience and love are antitheses of each other.

Also, patience is a demonstration of perseverance which, in the tradition of love, is the most contemptible of all and the worst indication of hostility as a poet has said:

He is good at demonstrating perseverance to the foes while finding incapacitation with the loved ones to be quite ugly.

From this onset, people who know the truth have said that patience is the most difficult station for people in general, the most undesirable along the path of love and the most uncommon along the path of *Tawhid* (oneness of Allah).

It is the hardest for the people in general because one is not trained on taming himself, nor is he placated with patience when afflicted, nor is he accustomed to self-control, so he cannot tolerate affliction, and he cannot be among the people of love so he may find pleasure in affliction. If the Truthful One, praise to Him, tests him with affliction, he cannot tolerate it and is overwhelmed by impatience, finding it hard to suppress himself from showing it because he does not feel comfortable with it.

It is the most undesirable along the path of love because love requires feeling comfortable in the presence of the loved one, finding pleasure in affliction because this means the presence of the one because of whom there is an affliction while preferring what the loved one wants, whereas patience requires hating affliction as indicated above, so there is a clash here.

It is most uncommon when it comes to *Tawhid* because one who perseveres claims the strength of firmness, the claim of steadfastness and the strength to withstand recklessness of the *nafs*. *Tawhid* requires the fusing of the *nafs*; so, it [patience] becomes the most uncommon because proving one's self in the path of *Tawhid* is the ugliest of abominations. Rather, surrender, despite its great station and loftiness among people who examine *Tawhid* is [only] among the first of its venues. This is so because their conduct is to fuse themselves into *Tawhid*. Surrender is the annihilation of one's will in order to submit to the will of the Truthful One, the most High, to truly stand with whatever Allah Almighty wants.

The distant stations between patience and acceptance have already been made clear to you: distant stations and tough paths.

Acceptance has three degrees arranged in strength the same way as they are in wording as follows:

The First Degree of Acceptance

One looks at the position of affliction, the action that necessitates acceptance, so he realizes its impact and feels its pain, yet he accepts it, even desires it, seeking it with his intellect even if his nature dislikes it. Such folks seek rewards of Allah Almighty for it, hoping for an increase in his nearness with Him and for winning Paradise the expanse of which is like that of the heavens and the earth, the one prepared for the pious.

This section of acceptance is relevant to the pious. An example for it is one seeking bloodletting and cupping from a doctor who is familiar with the details of his illnesses and what is required to heal him: He realizes that there is pain in this action, yet he accepts it, desires it, feeling greatly appreciative of the one who performs the bloodletting or cupping.

Also similar to it is one who travels seeking material gain: He realizes the hardship of travel, but his love for the fruit of his trip placates for him the hardship of traveling, accepting it. No matter what a calamity from Allah Almighty befalls him, being convinced that the reward stored for him by far exceeds his extreme expectations, he accepts it, desires it, loves it and thanks Allah Almighty for it.

The Second Degree of Acceptance

One also realizes the pain, yet he loves it because it is desired by the one whom he loves. One who is overpowered by love seeks and loves whatever pleases the one whom he loves. This exists as we see how people love each other. Such love has been described by those who express it in their poetry and prose. It only means noticing the outward picture with the eyes.

But this beauty is only skin on bones and love filled with filth and dirt: It starts from a contemptible drop of sperms, and it ends with a filthy stink, while one between this status and that keeps carrying his feces [wherever he goes].

One who looks at his lowly beauty does so with lowly eyes that err quite often about what they see: They see what is small as big and what is big as small, what is distant as near and what is ugly as beautiful.

If one imagines being controlled by this love, how could it be impossible for him to love the eternal perpetual beauty the perfection of which cannot be realized with one's foresight where erring is not possible, where death does not end such beauty but remains alive with Allah ﷻ after one dies happy and pleased with whatever Allah ﷻ sustained him, benefiting by death with more awareness and discovery. This is obvious when one contemplates on it, and it is supported by a host of religious literary legacy about the conditions and statements of those who love. Some of this legacy will, God willing, be quoted. This is the status of those who are near to Allah.

The Third Degree of Acceptance

One invalidates his sense of pain to the extent that what is painful happens to him, yet he does not feel it, and he is wounded yet he does not realize it.

An example for it is a warrior: When he is angry or afraid, a wound may afflict him, but he does not feel it till he sees blood gushing out, so he sees it as evidence that he was wounded. When someone runs because he has committed something dubious, so a thorn pierces through his foot, he does not feel the pain because his heart is occupied by something else. One who goes through cupping or shaves his head with something which causes pain does not feel the pain even after the person performing the cupping or the shaving finishes.

All this is due to the fact that when the heart (mind) is occupied with something, it does not realize or sense anything else besides it.

Similarities to it exist in the concerns of people of this life, in being busy with it, in coveting it, so much so that they do not feel the pain, the hunger, the thirst and the fatigue. There are many examples which one can see with his eyes: The one who is passionately in love and who is deeply immersed in looking at the one whom he/she loves. He may be afflicted by something which causes pain or grief, but due to his passion, he does not realize it because extreme love is taking control of his heart. All this is so when such pain or grief comes from someone else other than the one whom he/she loves; so, imagine if it comes from the one whom he/she loves!

The heart's preoccupation with love and passion is one of the strongest mental occupations. If you imagine this about light pain, imagine it about a great pain regarding a great love: Love, too, can be imagined as doubling many times in power just as pain can be imagined. When love for beautiful pictures can be strongly felt with the sense of vision, love for beautiful pictures can likewise be mentally visualized through the *nūr* (celestial light) of Divinely bestowed vision. Their greatness cannot be compared with any other greatness. One for whom a glimpse of it is revealed may be dazzled, so much so that he is stunned, and he enters into a swoon, not feeling what happens to him.

It is narrated that a woman stumbled, so her nail was removed. She smiled. She was asked, "Do you not feel the pain?" She said, "The pleasure of its reward has removed from my heart the bitterness of its pain."

Someone treated someone else of an illness which afflicted him. But he did not treat himself. He was asked about it, so he said, "Whatever pain is received because of the one you love is not painful at all."

Reference to a Group of Ancestors Whose Acceptance of Destiny as Transmitted by Scholars

Be informed that what we have stated in the chapter about patience from a group of prominent ones includes acceptance of destiny with regard to the death of sons and the like. Let us here mention general matters:

When the pain of [Prophet] Job, peace be with him, intensified, his wife said to him, "Why do you not supplicate to your Lord so He may remove your affliction?" He said to her, "Wife! I lived in power and prosperity for seventy years; so, I want now to live the same period in affliction, perhaps thus I will have thanked Allah for what He has blessed me, so patience is most befitting me for what He has tested me."[185]

It is also reported that Jonah (Prophet Yunus), peace be with him, said once to Gabriel, peace be with him, "Take me to the one who adores [his Maker] the most from among the people of the earth." He took him to a man whose hands and legs were cut off due to leprosy, and both his vision and hearing had gone, too, yet he kept saying, "Lord! You permitted me to enjoy them as long as You willed, and You have taken away whatever You will, keeping for me my hope in You, O most Kind, the One Who is the most connected with His servants!"[186]

It has also been narrated that Jesus, peace be with him, passed once by a man who was blind, leucodermic, handicapped, both his sides hit with

---

[185] This text is narrated with some wording variation in Vol. 1, p. 40 of *Tanbih Al-Khawatir* and on p. 127 of *Irshad Al-Qulub*.

[186] Al-Majlisi, *Bihar Al-Anwar*, Vol. 82, p. 153.

hemiplegia and his flesh scattered around him because of leprosy, yet the man kept saying, "Praise to Allah Who has healed me from what He has afflicted many from among His creation." Jesus, peace be with him, said to him, "Man! What affliction can I see that it has been kept away from you?!" The man said, "O Spirit of Allah! My condition is better than those in whose heart Allah did not place knowledge of Him which He has placed in mine." Jesus ﷺ said to him, "You have said the truth. Stretch your hand to me." The man stretched his hand to Jesus and instantly he was turned into the most beautiful of all people, having the best form, Allah having removed all his suffering. The man accompanied Jesus ﷺ and worshipped with him.[187]

Someone has narrated saying, "In my youth, I went to Abadan and saw a blind man who was also leprous, mentally retarded and epileptic. Ants were eating of his flesh. I raised his head and placed it in my lap with the desire to learn and repeat what he was saying. He woke up and said, 'Who is this busy-body who is intercepting my connection with my Lord? By Him do I swear that if He cuts me to pieces, I will never increase in anything but in more love for Him.'
Due to extreme itch, someone's leg was severed from the knee down. He said, "Praise be to Allah Who took away from me one (limb), leaving three. By Your Dignity! If you took away, you have kept. If you afflict, you heal." He did not miss a single act of adoration that night.

Someone said, "I have won from every station a position save acceptance of destiny. I have nothing of it except its smell. Despite this, if He permits all creations to enter Paradise while lodging me in hell, I will still be pleased with Him." A Gnostic once was told, "You have earned the extreme end of acceptance." He said, "No, I have not won the

---

[187] *Ibid.*

extreme end of acceptance but a status of acceptance; had Allah made me a bridge over hell on which all creations pass to Paradise, then He filled hell with me, I would still love His wisdom and accept His allotment for me."

This is the speech of one who knows that love has consumed his concern, preventing him from feeling the pain of fire. Such a status taking control of one's soul is not impossible, but it is distant with regard to weak conditions during this time, and a deprived weakling should not renounce the condition of the strong, thinking that what he is incapable of doing is also not doable by others.

Imran ibn Haseen, may Allah be pleased with him, suffered once from a stomach pain. He remained lying on his back for thirty years unable to stand up or even sit. A hole was made in his bed through which he would relieve himself as a toilet. His brother al-Alaa visited him and kept weeping for his condition. He said to his brother, "What are you weeping about?" He said, "I weep for seeing you in such an awful condition." He said, "Do not weep; if Allah loves it for me, I, too, love it." Then he said to his brother, "Let me tell you something perhaps Allah will make it beneficial for you, but I want you to keep it confidential till I die: The angels visit me, and I feel very comfortable with them. They greet me and I hear their greeting. Thus, I know that this affliction is not a penalty; it is the reason behind this great bliss. If one sees this [sight of the angels] in his affliction, why should he not be pleased with it?"

Some people have said, "We visited Suwaid ibn Shu'bah. We found a shirt thrown, but we did not think that there was anything underneath it till he removed it. His wife said to him, 'May your wife be sacrificed for your sake! Should we provide you with food or drink?' He said, 'My lying down has over-extended, the hipbones have become exhausted and worn out. I have not been eating or drinking since—and he stated the number of days—yet it does not please me for this status to disappear as much as a piece of clipped nail.'"

It has been narrated about someone who suffered acutely of sickness for sixty years. When his condition worsened, his sons visited him and said, "Do you wish to die so you may rest from your condition?" He said, "No." They said, "What do you, then, want?" He said, "I want nothing; I am only a slave, and only the Master has a will over His slave and the judgment."

It has also been said that the sickness of Fath al-Musilli intensified. Besides his sickness, he was afflicted with poverty and exhaustion. He said, "My Lord and Master! You afflicted me with ailment and poverty; such are Your deeds with the prophets and messengers; so, how can I thank You for the blessing which You have bestowed on me?"

Be informed that supplication repels affliction. The removal of ailment and the safeguarding of sons do not clash with accepting destiny. Allah, Glory belongs to Him, has ordered us to worship Him with supplication, urging and encouraging us to plead to Him and regarding the abandoning of supplication as a sign of haughtiness while doing it is an act of adoration, promising us to answer our pleas. He called on His Prophets and the Imams, peace be with them, to do likewise and to enjoin others to supplicate. Citations from their statements are innumerable. Allah Almighty has praised those among His servants who plead to Him saying, "**They used to call upon Us with love and fear** (love for rewards and fear of punishment)" (Qur'ān, 21:90).

3 - Acceptance

Among the obligations of the pleading person is that he, during his supplication, must be obedient to the command of his Lord, Blessed and Exalted is He, by pleading for what He has ordered him to plead. Had He not ordered him to plead for it, and had He not commanded him and permitted him to plead, he would not have dared to oppose His decree. In fact, this is a sort of acceptance for those who accept, those who discipline themselves, those who perform the obligations associated with supplication.

One of the marks of acceptance is that if his plea is not answered, he does not feel any pain because of that, for it is quite possible one pleads for something which, if granted, would bring him harm with which only Allah Almighty is familiar. It is also recorded that one may keep pleading to Allah Almighty for something to the extent that the angels sympathize with him, so they would say, "Lord! Have mercy on Your believing servant and answer his plea!" Allah Almighty will then say, "How shall I rid him of something with which I have mercy on him?"

Yes, if one feels apprehensive about the possibility that Allah Almighty did not answer his plea because he is distant from Him, something which brings about disappointment, presentiment, expulsion and exclusion, there is no harm in it, for a believer's perfection lies in his holding his *nafs* in contempt, looking at it as a low thing even if his plea is answered: He does not think that such an answer is due to his high status with Allah Almighty and his nearness to Him. Rather, this may be due to the contempt and hatred of Allah Almighty of his voice, from the angels being harmed by his stink, so they plead to Allah Almighty to speed up answering his plea so these angels may be relieved.

Also, the reason behind delaying answering the plea is due to Allah Almighty and His angels loving his voice, enjoying the pleasure of his silent pleas, so the angels ask Allah Almighty to delay answering it. Also, as reports have narrated, a believer is always between anticipation and apprehension: It is through them that good deeds stand, wrongdoings are avoided, and deeds that please the Almighty are desired.

4 - Weeping

Be informed that weeping by itself does not clash with perseverance or with accepting destiny; rather, it is a human norm of behavior, an indication of one's humanity, an expression of affection towards kinsfolk or a loved one; so, there is no harm in demonstrating it, nor is there any harm in getting out to the open as long as it does not contain conditions which bring about Wrath or show alarm and thus take away rewards, such as one tearing his garment or beating his face or beating on the thigh, etc.

It has been reported about the Prophet, peace and blessings of Allah be with him and his progeny, weeping during tragic times, and before him about Adam, peace be with him, and after him about his progeny and companions despite their acceptance, perseverance, and firmness. The first to weep was Adam, peace be with him, over his son Able ﷺ whom he eulogized in well-known verses of poetry, grieving for him a great deal. If anything is hidden, there is nothing hidden about Jacob (Ya'qūb), peace be with him, who wept over Joseph (Yūsuf) ﷺ till his eyes turned white out of grief for Yūsuf, Joseph, peace be with him.

Among famous narratives are those quoting Imam al-Sādiq, peace be with him, as saying, "[Imam] Zainul 'Ābidīn, peace be with him, wept over his father for forty years, fasting during the day and standing for prayers during the night. When it was time for him to break his fast, his servant would bring him food and drink, placing it in front of him as he would say, 'Eat, Master.' He would say, 'The [grand]son of the Messenger of Allah was hungry when he was killed. The [grand]son of the Messenger of Allah was thirsty when he was killed.' He would keep repeating these statements and weeps till his food becomes wet from his tears. He continued to do so till he joined Allah, the most Exalted One, the most Great."[188]

One of his slaves reported saying, "He [Imam Zainul 'Ābidīn] went out to the desert, so I followed him. I found him prostrating on a rough rock. I stood as I kept hearing his inhalation and weeping. I counted one thousand times his repeating this statement:

لا اله الا الله حقا حقا، لا اله الا الله تعبدا و رقا، لا اله الا الله ايمانا و صدقا

There is no god save Allah, truly it is true; There is no god save Allah, I worship Him and I am His slave; There is no god save Allah, I believe in it and it is true.'

Then he raised his head from his prostration; his beard and face were awash by his tears. I, therefore, said, 'Master! Is it not time yet for your grief to come to an end and to your weeping to be less?' He said to me, 'Woe on you! Jacob son of Isaac son of Abraham, peace be with them, was a prophet the son of a prophet and the grandson of a prophet. He had twelve sons. Allah kept one of them away from him, so he grew grey hair on account of his grief, his back was bent due to his sadness and his eyesight was gone because of his weeping even while his son was alive in the life of this world. And I saw my father, brother and

---

[188] *Al-Luhuf fi Qata Al-Tufuf*, p. 87.

seventeen of my family members slain; so, how can my grief come to an end, and how can my weeping decrease?!"[189]

Anas ibn Malik said once, "I went in the company of the Messenger of Allah, peace and blessings of Allah be with him and his progeny, to visit Abu Saif al-Qayn who was foster-father of Ibrahim [Abraham, son of the Prophet by his wife Mary the Copt]. The Messenger of Allah ﷺ took Ibrahim and kept kissing and smelling him. Then he went after that to visit him [Abu Saif al-Qayn] when Ibrahim, peace be with him, was drawing his last breath. The eyes of the Messenger of Allah, peace and blessings of Allah be with him and his progeny, kept shedding tears. Abdul-Rahman ibn Awf said to him, 'Even you, O Messenger of Allah [cry]?!' He ﷺ said, 'O son of Awf! It is mercy,' repeating his statement. Then the Messenger of Allah ﷺ said, 'The eye is tearful, the heart grieves, and we do not say anything but whatever pleases our Lord. We, on account of your parting, O Ibrahim, are grieved.'"[190]

Asmaa daughter of Zaid is quoted as having said that when the son of the Messenger of Allah, peace and blessings of Allah be with him and his progeny, namely Ibrahim, peace be with him, passed away, the Messenger of Allah ﷺ wept. Someone consoling him said to him, "You are the greatest in magnifying Allah's right, the most Exalted One, the most Great." The Messenger of Allah ﷺ said, "The eye sheds its tears, the heart grieves, and we do not say anything that brings the Wrath of the Lord. Had it not been a just destined promise, one that includes everyone [death], and the last one will follow the very first, we would

---

[189] *Ibid.*, p. 88.

[190] Al-Bukhari, *Sahih*, Vol. 2, p. 105.

have grieved for you in a way better than we already have and we, O Ibrahim, are grieved because of you."[191]

Jabir ibn Abdullah al-Ansari, may Allah be pleased with him, has said that the Messenger of Allah ﷺ took the hand of Abdul-Rahman ibn Awf and went to see Ibrahim as the latter was drawing his last breath. He placed Ibrahim in his lap and said to him, "O son! I cannot help you against the will of Allah in anything at all," shedding his tears. Abdul-Rahman said to him, "O Messenger of Allah! Do you weep?! Did you not prohibit weeping?" He ﷺ said, "I prohibited lamenting in two foolish and licentious sounds: the sound made on hearing a sporting tone, merry-making and Satan's windpipes, and the sound made on a calamity befalling: the scratching of cheeks, the tearing asunder of shirts, and the tone of Satan. But this [weeping is a sign of] mercy: One who is not merciful to others will not receive mercy [from the Almighty]. Had it not been a just matter, a true promise, a path which we all tread upon, our last will catch up with our first, we would have grieved more intensely than this; we are on your account [O Ibrahim] grieved; the eye is tearful, the heart is sad, and we do not say what angers the Lord, the most Exalted One, the most Great."[192]

Abu Umamah is quoted as having said that a man visited the Prophet ﷺ when his son [Ibrahim] had died and saw his eyes filled with tears, so he said, "O Prophet of Allah! Do you shed tears for this child?! I

---

[191] Ibn Majah, *Sunan*, Vol. 1, pp. 1506, 1589; *Muntakhab Kanzul-Ummal*, Vol. 6, p. 265.

[192] *Al-Taazi*, pp. 8-9 with a minor wording variation. It has been narrated in different wording in al-Tirmidhi's *Sunan*, Vol. 2, pp. 1011, 1237; and in *Al-Jaami' Al-Kabir*, Vol. 1, p. 290. Something similar to it is narrated in *Muntakhab Kanzul-Ummal*, Vol. 6, p. 265 from Abd ibn Hameed.

swear by the One Who sent you with the truth, I buried twelve sons during the time of Jahiliyya each and every one of them was younger than him. I tossed each one in the ground." The Prophet ﷺ said, "So what if mercy departed from you?! The heart is grieved, the eye is tearful, and we do not say anything that angers the Lord; we are over Ibrahim grieved."

Mahmoud ibn Labeed has said that an eclipse of the sun took place when Ibrahim son of the Messenger of Allah ﷺ died, so people said, "The sun has eclipsed for Ibrahim's death." The Messenger of Allah ﷺ, he went on, came out when he heard about it. He praised Allah and lauded him then said, "O people! The sun and the moon are two of the signs of Allah, the most Exalted One, the most Great, and they do not eclipse for the death or the life of anyone. If you see them eclipse, you must rush to the mosques to pray." Then his eyes were filled with tears. People said, "O Messenger of Allah! Do you weep while you are the Messenger of Allah?!" He ﷺ said, "I am only human; the eye sheds its tears; the heart senses the tragedy, and we do not say anything that angers the Lord. By Allah, O Ibrahim, we are grieved on your account."[193]

Khalid ibn Ma'dan is quoted as having said that when Ibrahim son of the Prophet ﷺ died, the Prophet ﷺ wept, so it was said to him, "O Messenger of Allah! Do you weep?!" He ﷺ said, "A fragrant flower which Allah gifted to me, and I used to smell it."

---

[193] Something similar to it is narrated in al-Kolayni's *Al-Kāfi*, Vol. 3, pp. 7, 208 from Ali ibn Abdullah ibn Abul-Hasan Mousa, peace e with him. It is also narrated in some variation in its wording by al-Mughirah ibn Shu'bah as recorded in al-Bukhari's *Sahih*, Vol. 2, pp. 42, 48 and by Muslim in his *Sahih*, Vol. 2, pp. 628, 630.

On the day when Ibrahim died, he ﷺ said, "Any grief in the heart or in the eye is mercy; grieving with the tongue or hand is an act of Satan."[194]

Al-Zubayr ibn Bakkar narrated saying that the Prophet ﷺ went out to bury [his son] Ibrahim. Then he sat on his grave. When he was taken down into the grave, the Messenger of Allah ﷺ saw him, so he wept. When the *sahaba* (companions) saw that, they, too, wept, so much so that their voices rose. Abu Bakr went to him and said, "O Messenger of Allah! Do you weep while prohibiting us from weeping?!" The Prophet ﷺ said, "The eye sheds its tears, the heart is in pain, and we do not say anything that angers the Lord, the most Exalted One, the most Great."

Al-Saaib ibn Yazid is quoted as having said that when al-Tahir son of the Prophet ﷺ passed away, the Prophet ﷺ wept, so it was said to him, "O Messenger of Allah! Have you really wept?!" He ﷺ said, "The eye sheds, the tear subdues, and the heart grieves; we do not disobey Allah, the most Exalted One, the most Great."[195]

In his *Sahih*, Muslim narrates saying that the Prophet ﷺ visited his mother's grave, so he wept and all those around him wept, too.[196]

It has also been narrated that when Othman ibn Maz'un died, the Prophet ﷺ uncovered the sheet to see his face; he kissed him on the forehead then wept for a long time. When the coffin was raised, he ﷺ

---

[194] *Al-Jaami' Al-Kabir*, Vol. 1, p. 709 with minor wording difference.

[195] This tradition is cited in *Al-Jami' Al-Kabir*, Vol. 1, p. 207.

[196] Muslim, *Sahih*, Vol. 2, p. 671; Al-Nisā'i, *Sunan*, Vol. 4, p. 90; Abu Dawud, *Sunan*, Vol. 3, pp. 218, 3234.

said, "Congratulations to you, O Othman! The world did not confuse you, nor did you confuse it."[197]

Sa`d ibn Abadah complained once [about being sick], so the Messenger of Allah ﷺ went to visit him. When he entered his room, he saw him in a coma. He ﷺ asked, "Has he died?" They said, "No, O Messenger of Allah." The Messenger of Allah ﷺ wept. When people saw how he wept, they, too, wept. He ﷺ said, "Do you not hear [me say this]? Allah does not torment one because of his eyes' tears, nor because his heart grieves. Rather, He torments because of this—pointing to his tongue—or He may show mercy."[198]

It has been narrated that the Messenger of Allah ﷺ received a message once about his granddaughter being sick. He ﷺ said, "To Allah belongs whatever He takes, and to Allah belongs whatever He gives." He ﷺ went to see her accompanied by some of his companions. The mother took out a little girl to him whose breath was irregular, so he ﷺ felt pity for her and his eyes poured down their tears. His companions looked at him [critically], so he ﷺ said, "What is wrong with you so you look at me like that? This is mercy [feeling of pity] which Allah places wherever He wills; Allah is merciful to those among His servants who are merciful to others."[199]

---

[197] This tradition is cited in *Al-Jami' Al-Kabir*, Vol. 1, p. 568.

[198] Al-Bukhari, *Sahih*, Vol. 2, p. 106. Muslim, *Sahih*, Vol. 2, pp. 636, 924 with minor wording difference.

[199] Al-Bukhari, *Sahih*, Vol. 2, p. 100, Vol. 7, p. 151, Vol. 8, p. 166 and Vol. 9, pp. 141, 164; Muslim, *Sahih*, Vol. 2, pp. 635, 923; *Al-Ta`azi*, p. 10; Ibn Majah, *Sunan*, Vol. 1, pp. 506, 1588; Abu Dawūd, *Sunan*, Vol. 3, pp. 193, 3125 and al-Nisā'i, *Sunan*, Vol. 4, p. 22 with a difference in its wording.

Usamah ibn Zaid is quoted as having said that Umama daughter of Zainab [daughter of Jahsh, cousin of the Prophet and later his wife] was brought to the Prophet ﷺ as her breath was quite irregular. He ﷺ said, "Whatever Allah takes belongs to Him, and whatever Allah gives is His; everyone is destined to see his day," then he wept. Sa`d ibn Abadah said, "Do you weep while you prohibited weeping?!" The Messenger of Allah ﷺ said, "It is mercy which Allah places in the heart of His servants; Allah is merciful unto those from among His servants who are merciful to each other."[200]

When Ja`far ibn Abu Talib, may Allah be pleased with him, was martyred, the Messenger of Allah ﷺ went to see Asmaa, may Allah be pleased with her. He said to her, "Get the children of Ja`far out for me." They came out, whereupon he ﷺ hugged and smelled them then shed tears. Asmaa asked him, "O Messenger of Allah! Has Ja`far been killed?" He ﷺ said, "Yes, he has been martyred today."[201]

Abdullah ibn Ja`far has said, "I recollect how the Messenger of Allah ﷺ visited my mother and eulogized to her the death of my father. She looked at him as he kept rubbing on my head and on that of my brother while his eyes were shedding their tears, so much so that his beard started dripping. Then he said, 'Lord! Ja`far went to receive the best reward; so, bestow Your blessing on his sons in the very best way in which You have done for any of Your servants.' Then he ﷺ said, 'O Asmaa! Shall I give you some glad tiding?" She said, "Yes, please, may both my parents be sacrificed for your sake!' He said, 'Allah Almighty has made two wings for Ja`far whereby he flies in Paradise.'"

---

[200] Ahmed, *Musnad*, Vol. 5, pp. 204, 207 with a minor wording difference.
[201] Al-Waqidi, *Al-Maghazi*, Vol. 2, p. 766 with a minor wording variation.

4 - Weeping

Abi-Abdillah (The father of Abdullah: Imam Husayn), peace be with him, quotes his father who quotes the Prophet ﷺ saying that when he came to know that Ja`far ibn Abu Talib, may Allah be pleased with him, and Zaid ibn Harithah were martyred, he mourned them both whenever he entered his home. He said, "They both used to talk to me and entertain me, then death took them away."[202]

Khalid ibn Salamah has said that when the Prophet ﷺ came to know about the death of Zaid ibn Harithah, he went to Zaid's house where a small daughter of Zaid came out to him. When she saw the Messenger of Allah ﷺ, she scratched her face [in grief], whereupon the Messenger of Allah ﷺ wept and sobbed, so he was asked, "What is this [that you are doing], O Messenger of Allah?!" He said, "It is the [crying of a] lover feeling anxious about the one he loves."[203]

When Sa`d ibn Mu`adh, may Allah be pleased with him, died, the Messenger of Allah ﷺ wept a great deal.

He ﷺ once said the following to the mother of Sa`d ibn Mu'adh: "Will your tears dry and your grief subside, for the Arsh (Allah's throne) has shaken on account of your son?"

It is said that the Messenger of Allah ﷺ would weep, and he would wipe his face, but no sound would come out of him."[204]

---

[202] *Al-Faqih*, Vol. 1, pp. 113, 527 with a minor wording difference.
[203] *Makarim Al-Akhlaq*, p. 22.
[204] Ahmed, *Musnad*, Vol. 4, p. 456; *Al-Mustadrak ala Al-Sahihain*, Vol. 3, p. 206; *Al-Jami' Al-Kabir*, Vol. 1, p. 360.

Al-Baraa ibn `Azib is quoted as having said, "While we were in the company of the Messenger of Allah, peace and blessings of Allah with him and his progeny, he saw a group of people, so he said, 'Why have these folks gathered together like that?' He was told that they were digging a grave. The Messenger of Allah ﷺ immediately went out from among his companions in a hurry and knelt down on the grave. I faced him in order to see what he would do. He wept till the ground became wet from his tears, then he addressed us saying, 'Brothers! It is for the like of this that you should be prepared.'"[205]

He ﷺ has also said, "Nobody has control over his grief; it is an expression of affection for one's brother."[206]

When the Prophet ﷺ returned from Uhud to Medina, he was met by Hamna daughter of Jahsh. People offered condolences to her on the occasion of the martyrdom of her brother Abdullah ibn Jahsh. She said, "*Inna Lillahi wa Inna Ilayhi Raji'oon* (We belong to Allah, and to Him shall we return)." She prayed the Almighty to forgive him. Then people consoled her on the martyrdom of her uncle Hamzah, so she said, "*Inna Lillahi wa Inna Ilayhi Raji'oon* (We belong to Allah, and to Him shall we return)." She prayed the Almighty to forgive him, too. Then she was consoled on the martyrdom of her husband Mus`ab ibn `Umayr, whereupon she cried and wailed; therefore, the Messenger of Allah ﷺ said, "A woman's husband surely has a special status with her" due to

---

[205] Ahmed, *Musnad*, Vol. 4, p. 294. Something like it is narrated in Ibn Majah's *Musnad*, Vol. 3, pp. 1403, 4195.

[206] *Al-Jami' Al-Saghir*, Vol. 2, pp. 113, 5135. It is narrated with minor wording variation in *Al-Durr Al-Manthur*, Vol. 1, p. 158.

his having witnessed how she persevered about the death of her brother and uncle and how she cried over her husband.²⁰⁷

Then the Messenger of Allah ﷺ passed by the homes of the Ansar from among Banu Abd al-Ashhal. He heard weeping and wailing over those who had been killed [during the battle of Uhud], so his eyes were immediately tearful, and he wept. Then he said, "But Hamzah has none to weep over him..." When Sa`d ibn Mu`adh and Aseed ibn Hudair returned to the homes of Banu al-Ashhal, they both ordered their women to go and mourn the uncle of the Prophet ﷺ [Hamzah]. When the Prophet ﷺ heard their weeping over Hamzah, he came out to them as they were at the mosque's gate crying. He ﷺ said to them, "Go back, may Allah have mercy on you; you have indeed consoled in person."

The mentor narrates in his *Tahdhib*, through *isnad* traced back to Imam al-Sādiq, peace be with him, saying that "Ibrahim (Abraham), Friend of the most Merciful One, pleaded to his Lord to grant him a daughter who would mourn him after his death."²⁰⁸

Ibn Mas`ūd is quoted as having said that the Messenger of Allah ﷺ said, "One who slaps cheeks and tears garments does not belong to us."²⁰⁹

---

²⁰⁷ Ibn Hisham, *Seera*, Vol. 3, p. 104.
²⁰⁸ *Al-Tahdhib*, Vol. 1, pp. 465, 1524.
²⁰⁹ Ahmed, *Musnad*, Vol. 1, p. 386; Al-Bukhari, *Sahih*, Vol. 2, p. 104; Muslim, *Sahih*, Vol. 1, pp. 99, 165; Ibn Majah, *Sunan*, Vol. 1, pp. 504, 1584; Al-Nisaa'i, *Sunan*, Vol. 4, pp. 20, 21; Al-Majlisi, *Bihar Al-Anwar*, Vol. 82, pp. 93, 45.

Abu Umamah has said that the Messenger of Allah ﷺ said, "May the Almighty curse one who scratches her face, who tears her garment, who wails and laments."[210]

He ﷺ is quoted as having prohibited people from walking behind a coffin while wailing and weeping.[211]

Amr ibn Shu'ayb quotes his father quoting his grandfather saying that it is very much held in contempt by the Almighty when one eats while not being hungry, sleeps without having stayed late at night, laughs without having seen something unusual, makes a noise of wailing when calamity falls, and blows a windpipe when prosperous."[212]

Yahya ibn Khalid has said that a man went to see the Prophet ﷺ. He asked him, "What voids rewards at the time when calamity befalls someone?" The Prophet ﷺ said, "It is when someone slaps one hand with the other; when one is first afflicted, if he accepts it, he, too, will be accepted [by the Almighty], and if he is wrathful, wrath shall fall upon him."[213]

Umm Salamah, may Allah be pleased with her, has said, "When Abu Salamah, may Allah be pleased with him, died a stranger in a strange land, I said that I would cry over him in a way which people will talk about. I was about to cry when a woman came with the intention to entertain me, so the Messenger of Allah ﷺ welcomed her and said, 'Do

---

[210] *Al-Jami' Al-Saghir*, Vol. 2, pp. 405, 7252; Ibn Majah, *Sunan*, Vol. 1, pp. 505, 1585; Al-Majlisi, *Bihar Al-Anwar*, Vol. 83, p. 93.

[211] Ibn Majah, *Sunan*, Vol. 1, pp. 504, 1583.

[212] *Al-Jami' Al-Saghir*, Vol. 2, pp. 268, 6216.

[213] *Bihar Al-Al-Anwar*, Vol. 82, p. 93.

you want to permit Satan to enter a house from which Allah kicked him out?' I, therefore, did not proceed with crying."

Imam al-Baqir is quoted as having said, "The severest form of one's alarm status is screaming while weeping and wailing, slapping the face and chest, pulling the hair. When one resorts to wailing, he abandons patience; one who demonstrates patience, says *'Inna Lillahi wa Inna Ilayhi Raji'oon'* (We belong to Allah, and to Him is our return), praising Allah, Great is His Mention and accepts what Allah does, his rewards will be with Allah, the most Exalted, the most Great One. One who does not do that will be subjected to destiny while being held in contempt, and Allah, the most Exalted, the most Great, will void his rewards."[214]

Imam al-Sādiq has said that the Messenger of Allah said, "If one beats with his hand his thigh, he voids his rewards."[215]

---

[214]*Al-Kāfi*, Vol. 3, pp. 1, 222.

[215]*Al-Kāfi*, Vol. 3, pp. 4, 224 with a minor wording variation.

Significance of saying *"Inna Lillahi wa Inna Ilayhi Raji'oon*

It is recommended, when calamity befalls someone, that the latter should say: *Inna Lillahi wa Inna Ilayhi Raji'oon* (We belong to Allah, and to Him shall we return).

Allah Almighty has said,

الَّذِينَ إِذَا أَصَابَتْهُمْ مُصِيبَةٌ قَالُوا إِنَّا لِلَّهِ وَإِنَّا إِلَيْهِ رَاجِعُونَ ۞ الَّذِينَ إِذَا أَصَابَتْهُمْ مُصِيبَةٌ قَالُوا إِنَّا لِلَّهِ وَإِنَّا إِلَيْهِ رَاجِعُونَ

"... [Those] who say, when afflicted with calamity, 'To Allah do we belong, and to Him do we return' are the ones on whom God's blessings and mercy (descend), and they are the ones who receive guidance" (Qur'ān, 2:156-7).

The Prophet ﷺ has said, "If one has four merits, the greatest *nūr* of Allah will be in him: one who sets his reliance on his testimony that There is no god save Allah and that I am the Messenger of Allah, one who, when afflicted with a calamity, says *Inna Lillahi wa Inna Ilayhi Raji'oon* (We belong to Allah, and to Him shall we return), one who, when he earns something good, says *Alhamdu-Lillah* (Praise belongs to Allah), and one who, on committing a sin, says *Astaghfirullaha wa Atūbu Ilayh* (I seek Allah's forgiveness, and I repent to Him)."[216]

Imam al-Baqir ؏ is quoted as having said, "Whenever a believer is afflicted with a calamity in the life of this world and says *Inna Lillahi wa Inna Ilayhi Raji'oon* (We belong to Allah, and to Him shall we return) when overwhelmed by the calamity, if he perseveres upon being

---

[216] *Al-Faqih*, Vol. 1, pp. 514, 111; *Al-Khisal*, pp. 49, 222.

hit by the calamity…, Allah will forgive his past sins except major ones for which Allah Almighty mandated the penalty of the fire. Whenever in the future he remembers a calamity that had befallen him and he says *Inna Lillahi wa Inna Ilayhi Raji'oon* (We belong to Allah, and to Him shall we return) at that time, praises Allah, the most Exalted and the most Great, Allah will forgive every sin which he had committed between the first time and the latter time of saying the mentioned supplication, except major sins."[217]

Both these traditions have been narrated by al-Sadūq. Al-Kolayni has rendered their *isnad* to Ma`ruf ibn Kharbudh citing Imam al-Baqir ﷺ without mentioning the exception referred to above with regard to major sins.[218]

Al-Kolayni, through his *isnad* to Dawud ibn Zirbi cites al-Sādiq ﷺ as saying, "If one remembers his sin, even after a long while, and says انا لله و انا اليه راجعون، و الحمد لله رب العالمين؛ اللهم أجرني على مصيبتي، و أخلف علي أفضل منها

Inna Lillahi wa Inna Ilayhi Raji'oon, Alhamdu-Lillahi Rabbil `Aalamin, Allahomma Ajirni ala Musibati wa Akhlif Alayya Afdala Minha (We belong to Allah, and to Him shall we return, praise belongs to Allah, Lord of the Worlds; Lord! Grant me rewards for my calamity and compensate me with something better than it), he will have the same reward which he had received when he was first afflicted."[219]

Muslim has quoted Umm Salamah, may Allah be pleased with her, saying that the Messenger of Allah ﷺ enjoined saying, "Any Muslim

---

[217] *Al-Faqih*, Vol. 1, pp. 111, 515.
[218] *Al-Kāfi*, Vol. 3, pp. 5, 224.
[219] *Ibid.*, Vol. 3, pp. 6, 224.

who is afflicted by a calamity and who says as he has been commanded by Allah *Inna Lillahi wa Inna Ilayhi Raji'oon, Alhamdu-Lillahi Rabbil `Aalamin,*: اللهم أجرني على مصيبتي، و أخلف علي أفضل منها *Allahomma Ajirni ala Musibati wa Akhlif Alayya Afdala Minha* (We belong to Allah, and to Him shall we return, praise belongs to Allah, Lord of the Worlds; Lord! Grant me rewards for my calamity and compensate me with something better than it), Allah will surely compensate me for that calamity with something good. When Abu Salamah died, I said, 'Who among the Muslims is better than Abu Salamah?! His was the first family that migrated to the Messenger of Allah; I made the statement, so Allah compensated me with the Messenger of Allah, peace and blessings of Allah be with him and his progeny."[220]

Al-Tirmidhi has narrated through his *isnad* to the Messenger of Allah ﷺ saying, "When the son of a servant of Allah dies, Allah Almighty would say to His angels, 'Have you taken the soul away of the son of My servant?' They would answer in the affirmative. He would say, 'Have you taken away the fruit of his heart?' They would again answer in the affirmative. He would then say, 'What did My servant say?' They would answer by saying, 'He praised You, said *Inna Lillahi wa Inna Ilayhi Raji'oon* (We belong to Allah, and to Him is our return).' The Almighty would then say, 'Build My servant a home in Paradise and call it بيت الحمد *Bayt al-Hamd*, Home of the Praise.'"[221]

A similar tradition is narrated by al-Kolayni from Imam al-Sādiq ﷺ who quotes the Prophet ﷺ.[222]

---

[220] Muslim, *Sahih*, Vol. 2, pp. 631, 918.

[221] Al-Tirmidhi, *Sunan*, Vol. 2, pp. 243, 1026.

[222] *Al-Kāfi*, Vol. 3, pp. 4, 218.

5 – On Mourning

Mourning is permissible with good praise, the enumeration of one's virtues while employing truthfulness because Fatima al-Zahra, peace be with her, did so when she said,

"يا أبتاه، من ربه ما أدناه! يا أبتاه! يا جبرائيل أنعاه! يا أبتاه! أجاب ربا دعاه"

O father! How close he is to his Lord! O father! To Gabriel do I mourn him. O father! One who responded when his Lord called on him."[223]

It is narrated that she took a handful of the dust of his grave, peace, and blessings of Allah with him and his progeny, and placed it on her eyes then composed this poetry:

ماذا على من شم تربة أحمد	أن لا يشم مدى الزمان غواليا؟
صبت علي مصائب لو أنها	صبت على الأيام صرن لياليا

What harm is there if one sniffs Ahmed's soil?

---

[223] *Dhikra Al-Shi'a*, p. 72; *I'lam Al-Wara*, p. 143; *Muntaha Al-Matlab*, Vol. 1, p. 466; Al-Bukhari, *Sahih*, Vol. 6, p. 18; *Al-Mustadrak ala Al-Sahihain*, Vol. 1, p. 382; Al-Nisaai, *Sunan*, Vol. 4, p. 13; Ibn Majah, *Sunan*, Vol. 1, pp. 30, 522.

That he forever never smells dear ones at all?
Calamities were poured on me had they been
Poured on days, they would have been turned into nights.[224]

It has already been stated how the Prophet ﷺ ordered [his uncle] Hamzah to be eulogized.

Abu Hamzah quotes Imam al-Baqir ؏ saying, "The son of al-Mughirah died, so Umm Salamah asked the Prophet ﷺ to permit her to go to mourn him, and he ﷺ did so; he was her cousin. She said these lines:

أنعى الوليد بن الوليد	أبا الوليد، فتى العشيرة
حامي الحقيقة ماجدا	يسمو الى طلب الوتيرة
قد كان غيثا للسنين	و جعفرا غدقا و ميرة

I mourn the son of his father, the father of his son, the youth of the tribe,
Protector of the truth, glorious, one who aspires to reach the peak.
He was the relief during bad years, the brimful river, the rations.

The narrative continues to say that the Messenger of Allah ﷺ did not find anything wrong with what she did, nor did he make any comment.[225]

---

[224] *Dhikra Al-Shi'a*, p. 72; *Al-Mu'tabar*, Vol. 1, p. 344; *Muntaha Al-Matlab*, Vol. 1, p. 466.

[225] *Al-Kāfi*, Vol. 5, pp. 2, 117; *Al-Tahdhib*, pp. 358, 1027 with minor wording variation.

Ibn Babawayh has narrated saying that Imam al-Baqir ﷺ stated in his will that he should be mourned during the pilgrimage season for ten years.[226]

Younus ibn Ya`qub quotes Imam al-Sādiq ﷺ as saying, "[Imam] Abu Ja`far, peace be with him, has said to me, 'Take out of my wealth such-and-such for female mourners who should mourn me for ten years at Mina during the time when pilgrims stay there.'"[227]

The companions said, the reason is to attract people's attention to the Imam's merits and raise the status of such merits so that people may emulate them and so people may know the status of the members of this Household, peace and blessings be with them, in order to follow in their footsteps especially since *taqiyya* (hiding beliefs in fear) is removed after death..., mourning someone by attributing what is wrong is prohibitive. Such mourning will be counting merits which do not exist. Also prohibitive is stranger men hearing the voice of women mourning, and so is slapping and scratching the cheeks, hair pulling and such behavior. It is on this premise that wailing is prohibited.

The Prophet ﷺ has said, "I dissociate myself from anyone who shaves [his moustache and beard] and who pulls his/her hair and raises his/her voice (during mourning)."[228]

---

[226] *Al-Faqih*, Vol. 1, pp. 116, 547.

[227] *Al-Kāfi*, Vol. 5, pp. 1, 117; *Al-Tahdhib*, Vol. 6, pp. 358, 1025.

[228] Muslim, *Sahih*, Vol. 1, p. 100; Al-Nisaai, *Sunan*, Vol. 4, p. 20; Ibn Majah, *Sunan*, Vol. 1, p. 505; *Al-Jami` Al-Saghir*, Vol. 1, pp. 415, 2709.

Speaking to Fatima, peace be with her, when [her cousin] Ja`far ibn Abu Talib was killed, he ﷺ said, "Do not wail or lament, and whatever I have said, I have articulated nothing but the truth."[229]

Abu Malik al-Ash`ari quotes the Prophet ﷺ as saying, "If the wailing woman does not repent, she will be resurrected on the Judgment Day wearing a shawl of tar."[230]

Abu Sa'eed al-Khudri is quoted as having said that the Messenger of Allah ﷺ condemned the wailing woman and the one who listens to her."[231]

He ﷺ is also quoted as having said, "One who slaps the cheeks [in agony] and tears clothes is none of us."[232]

This prohibition is understood to apply to what is regarded as wrongdoing, and this is the common denominator between it and the previous reports.

As regarding how to conclude such a loss, there are useful benefits in it which include the following:

---

[229] *Al-Faqih*, Vol. 1, pp. 116, 547.

[230] *Al-Khisal*, p. 226; Ahmed, *Musnad*, Vol. 5, p. 342; Muslim, *Sahih*, Vol. 2, pp. 644, 934; Ibn Majah, *Sunan*, Vol. 1, pp. 504, 1582; *Al-Mustadrak*, Vol. 1, p. 383; *Al-Targhib wal Tarhib*, Vol. 4, pp. 12, 351.

[231] Ahmed, Musnad, Vol. 3, p. 65; Abu Dawud, *Sunan*, Vol. 3, pp. 194, 3128; *Al-Jami` Al-Saghir*, Vol. 2, pp. 408, 7271; *Al-Targhib wal Tarhib*, Vol. 4, pp. 13, 351; *Al-Futuhat Al-Rabbaniyya*, Vol. 4, p. 129.

[232] Ibn Majah, *Sunan*, Vol. 1, pp. 504, 1584.

5 – On Mourning

It is highly commendable to offer condolences to the family of the deceased, actually it is for certain commendable. It is offering a consolation and an advice to take to patience when afflicted by calamities. It is meant to distract one's attention from the calamity and persevere rather than surrender to grief and depression. The way to do that is to surrender to the command of Allah, the most Sublime, the most Great, and to attribute what has happened to His justice and wisdom. And it is by remembering the rewards which Allah has promised those who persevere and praying for the deceased person and consoling the grieved person by taking his mind away from his calamity. There are many traditions about recommending it and urging the believers to do it:

Amr ibn Shu'ayb quotes his father quoting his grandfather saying that the Messenger of Allah ﷺ said once, "Do you know what rights a neighbor has on his neighbor? It is taking to assist him when he seeks help, to loan him when he asks for a loan, to visit him when impoverished, to console him when afflicted by a calamity, to congratulate him when something good happens to him, to visit him when he falls sick, to walk behind his coffin when he dies, not to build the house higher than his and thus block the movement of wind except with his permission, to give him a gift when you buy fruits, and if you do not do so, let it reach him discreetly. Do not let your children show it off to his children and thus cause them to be angry. Do not let him envy you for wealth coming your way except that you take a measure of it and give it to him."[233]

Bahz ibn Hakim ibn Mu'awiyah ibn Jidah al-Qushayri quotes his father quoting his grandfather saying, "I said [to the Messenger of Allah ﷺ],

---

[233] *Al-Targhib wal Tarhib*, Vol. 3, pp. 20, 357.

'O Messenger of Allah, what rights does my neighbor have on me?' He ﷺ said, 'When he falls sick, you should visit him...,' and he kept counting the same as above."[234]

As the rewards for it, Ibn Mas`ūd quotes the Prophet ﷺ as saying, "One who consoles someone afflicted by a calamity will receive the same rewards which the first receives."[235]

Jabir ibn Abdullah [al-Ansari], may Allah be pleased with him, has said that the Messenger of Allah ﷺ said, "One who consoles someone who has been afflicted with a calamity will receive the same rewards which he receives without diminishing any of his rewards[236]; one who shrouds a Muslim will be outfitted by Allah with **bracelets of gold, green garments of fine silk and heavy brocade (Qur'ān, 18:31)**; Allah will build a house in Paradise for one who digs a grave for a Muslim, and when one brings about ease to one suffering from a hardship will be shaded by Allah on a Day when there will be no shade save His."

Jabir also quotes the Prophet ﷺ as saying, "One who offers condolences to a bereaved person will be outfitted by Allah, the most Exalted One, the most Great, with outfits of piety, and He will bless his soul among the souls He blesses."[237]

The Prophet ﷺ was asked about handshaking during offering condolences. He said, "It brings comfort to the believer; one who

---

[234] *Al-Targhib wal Tarhib*, Vol. 3, p. 357, in the footnote to Tradition No. 20.

[235] *Al-Jami' Al-Kabir*, Vol. 1, p. 801.

[236] *Al-Kāfi*, Vol. 3, pp. 4, 227 from Abu Abdullah, peace be with him who cites the Messenger of Allah (ص).

[237] *Al-Jami` Al-Kabir*, Vol. 1, p. 801.

consoles an afflicted person will receive rewards equal to that of the afflicted person."

Abdullah ibn Abu Bakr ibn Muhammed ibn Omer ibn Hazm quotes his father quoting his grandfather saying that he heard the Messenger of Allah ﷺ saying, "One who visits a sick person remains in mercy, and when he sits by his side, he will be drenched into it. When he stands up to return, he keeps wading in it till he reaches the place from which he had come out. If one consoles his believing brother on account of a calamity, Allah, the most Exalted One, the most Great, will outfit him of the outfits of dignity on the Judgment Day."[238]

Abu Barzah has said that the Messenger of Allah ﷺ said, "One who consoles a widow will be outfitted with the outfits of Paradise."[239]

Anas [ibn Malik] has said that the Messenger of Allah (ص) said, "One who consoles his believing brother on a calamity will be outfitted by Allah, the most Exalted One, the most Great, with green outfits for which he will be envied on the Judgment Day."[240]

It has been narrated that Prophet Dawud (David), peace be with him, said, "Lord! What is the reward of one who consoles the grieved, the one who has been afflicted, seeking to please You?" He said, "His reward is that I outfit him with one of the outfits of *iman*(faith) with which I shield him from the Fire and get him to enter Paradise." He said, "Lord! What then is the reward of one who walks behind coffins seeking Your pleasure?" He said, "His reward is that the angels will

---

[238] *Ibid.*, Vol. 1, p. 800.

[239] Al-Tirmidhi, *Sunan*, Vol. 2, pp. 269, 1082.

[240] *Al-Jami` Al-Kabir*, Vol. 1, p. 801.

escort him on the day he dies to his grave, and I shall bless his soul among the souls I bless."²⁴¹

It has been narrated that Prophet Musa (Moses), peace be with him, asked his Lord once, "What reward shall one who visits a sick person receive?" He said, "I shall send at the time of his death angels who escort him to his grave who entertain him till the Gathering Day." He said, "Lord! What rewards does a person who consoles a woman who has lost her son receive?" He said, "I shall shade him with My shade—i.e., the shade of His Arsh—on the Day when there is no shade but Mine."²⁴²

It has also been reported that Prophet Ibrahim (Abraham) asked his Lord once, "Lord! What is the reward of one who wets his face with the tears of fearing You?" He said, "My blessings and Pleasure will be with him." He said, "Then what is the reward of one who commends a grieved person to take to patience seeking Your Pleasure?" He said, "I shall outfit him with the outfits of *iman*(faith) in which he enters Paradise and shuns the Fire." He said, "What then is the reward of one who supports a widow seeking Your Pleasure?" He said, "I shall keep him in My shade and lodge him in My Paradise." He said, "What is the reward of one who walks behind a coffin seeking to please You?" He said, "My angels shall bless his body and escort his soul."

---

²⁴¹ *Al-Durr Al-Manthur*, Vol. 5, p. 308. It is also narrated by al-Muttaqi al-Hindi in *Kanzul-Ummal*, Vol. 6, p. 355 with a difference in wording it.
²⁴² It is narrated by al-Kolayni in the second section of the *hadith* in *Al-Kāfi*, Vol. 3, pp. 1, 226 with minor variation.

5 – On Mourning

How To Console

Reports about handshaking in this regard have already been stated above.

As regarding what is agreed about in reference to the statements made and the reports dealing with offering consolations, there is nothing better in this dissertation to state more than what is recorded here, for in the following there is healing for what is in the hearts and sufficient wisdom in achieving these matters:

Imam Ali, peace be with him, has said, "Whenever the Messenger of Allah (ص) wanted to offer condolences to someone, he would say, 'آجرکم الله و رحمکم May Allah reward and have mercy on you.' And whenever he wanted to congratulate someone, he would say, 'بارك الله لکم، و بارك علیکم May Allah bless it for you, and may He shower His blessings on you.'"

It has been narrated that when a son was lost to Mu`adh, the latter's grief intensified, so much so that the Prophet ﷺ came to hear about it, so he wrote him saying, "In the Name of Allah, the most Gracious, the most Merciful. This is from Muhammed, the Messenger of Allah, to Mu'adh. Peace be with you. I praise Allah, the One and only God; may Allah magnify your rewards, instill in you patience and bless us and yourself with thanking Him, for our lives, those of our families and masters, in addition to those of our sons..., are all among Allah's enjoyable gifts, the most Exalted One, the most Great, the treasured trusts which we enjoy for a known term, and they are taken away at a certain time. He has enjoined us to thank Him when He grants us, to be patient when He tries us. Your son was one of the enjoyable gifts of Allah and treasured trusts. Allah permitted you to enjoy him gladly and happily, and He took him away from you in return for a great deal of rewards: prayers, mercy, and guidance if you persevere and place your trust in Him; so, do not combine two calamities lest your reward will be voided, and you will then regret what you have missed. If you see the rewards for your calamity, you will come to know that the calamity dwarfs besides Allah's rewards; therefore, rest your hope on Allah fulfilling His promise [of rewarding you], and let your sorrow for what has afflicted you be gone, as if there was no affliction at all, and peace [be with you]."[243]

Abu Abdullah, Imam Ja`far son of Imam Muhammed al-Sādiq, peace be with them both, quotes his father quoting his grandfather saying, "When the Messenger of Allah died, Gabriel, peace be with him, came to him as the Prophet was lying in state on the ground. Ali, Fatima, al-Hasan, and al-Husayn were in the house. Gabriel said to them, '*Assalāmu Alaykum*, Household of the Prophet; **Every soul shall have a taste of death: And only on the Day of Judgment shall you be paid your full recompense (Qur'ān, 3:185)**. Indeed, there is in Allah a solace from every calamity; everyone who dies shall be succeeded; everything that passes by shall be retracted; so, seek strength from Allah, the most Exalted One, the most Great; rest your hope on Him, for the true calamity is when one is deprived of the reward; this is the last time Gabriel descends to earth'."[244]

Jabir ibn Abdullah al-Ansari, Allah be pleased with him, has said, "When the Messenger of Allah passed away, the angels offered them

---

[243] This tradition is narrated in different wordings in *Al-Taazi*, pp. 12, 14; *Muntakhab Kanzul-Ummal*, Vol. 6, p. 277 and in *Al-Mustadrak ala Al-Sahihain*, Vol. 3, p. 273.

[244] *Al-Kāfi*, Vol. 3, pp. 5, 221; Al-Majlisi, *Bihar Al-Anwar*, Vol. 82, pp. 47, 96.

[Prophet's family] condolences; they heard voices but could not see who were behind them. They said, '*Assalamu Alaykum, O Ahl al-Bayt, wa Rahmatullahi wa Barakatuh*; indeed, there is in Allah, the most Exalted One, the most Great, solace from every calamity and compensation for whatever is missed; so, seek strength from Allah, on Him should you rest your hope, for the depraved one is that who is deprived of the rewards, *Wassalamu Alaykum wa Rahmatullahi wa Barakatuh*.'"[245]

Al-Bayhaqi, in *Al-Dalaa'il*, has said that when the Messenger of Allah ﷺ passed away, his companions looked at him and wept, having assembled around him. A man whose beard had more grey hair than black came in, and his bodily form was large and was good looking. He passed by them and wept. Then he turned to the companions of the Messenger of Allah ﷺ and said, "In Allah there is, indeed, consolation from every calamity and a recompense for whatever is left behind, and He succeeds whoever perishes; so, return to Allah, desire Him, for He looks at you when you are afflicted; therefore, you, too, look up to Him, for the true calamity is when one is not rewarded." Then he went away. Companions asked each other if they knew who the man was. Imam Ali, peace be with him, said, "Yes; he is the brother of the Messenger of Allah ﷺ, al-Khidhr, peace be with him."[246]

---

[245] *Al-Kāfi*, Vol. 3, pp. 6, 221 with a variation in its wording citing Imam Abu Abdullah, peace be with him; *Bihar Al-Anwar*, Vol. 82, p. 96.

[246] *Dalaa'il Al-Nubuwwah*, Vol. 7, p. 269; it is also narrated by al-Hakim in his *Mustadrak*, Vol. 3, p. 58, and by al-Majlisi in his *Bihar Al-Anwar*, Vol. 82, p. 97.

Mourning on the loss of loved ones

Ibn Abbas, may Allah be pleased with him, is quoted as having said that the Messenger of Allah ﷺ said, "If any of you is afflicted by a calamity, let him remember the calamity that afflicted me, for it is the most serious of all calamities."[247]

He ﷺ has also said, "One who sees his calamity as being great should remember his calamity in my regard, for his will then seem tolerable."

He ﷺ has also said during his sickness which eventually led to his demise, "O people! Any servant of Allah who is afflicted after my death with a calamity, let him seek solace in my regard [with my own death] to divert himself from any other calamity, for no member of my nation will ever be afflicted with a calamity harder on him than my own."[248]

Abdullah son of al-Walid, through his own *isnad*, says that "When Ali, peace be with him, was wounded, al-Hasan ؑ dispatched me to al-Husayn, peace be with them, when al-Husayn ؑ was in the Madaain [as its provincial governor]. When al-Husayn ؑ read the letter [sent to him by his revered wounded father ؑ], he said, 'What a calamity! How serious this calamity is! Yet the Messenger of Allah, peace and blessings of Allah be with him and his progeny, had said, 'If one of you is afflicted

---

[247] *Al-Kāfi*, Vol. 3, pp. 1, 220 with a variation of its wording from Imam Abu Abdullah [al-Sadiq], peace be with him; *Al-Jami' Al-Kabir*, Vol. 1, p. 41; *Al-Jami` Al-Saghir*, Vol. 1, p. 72.

[248] *Al-Jami` Al-Kabir*, Vol. 1, p. 372 with a difference in its wording; *Bihar Al-Anwar*, Vol. 82, p. 143.

5 – On Mourning

by a calamity, let him remember my calamity, for he shall never be afflicted with a calamity greater than it.'"[249]

Ishaq ibn Ammar quotes Imam al-Sādiq ﷺ as saying to him, "O Ishaq! Do not count a calamity for which you are granted patience and deserved rewards from Allah, the most Exalted One, the most Great, as a calamity; rather, a true calamity is one the person afflicted by it is deprived of its rewards because he did not take to patience when it descended on him."[250]

Abu Maysarah (or al-Fudail ibn Maysar, according to *Al-Kafi*) has said, "We were in the company of [Imam al-Sādiq ﷺ] Abu Abdullah, peace be with him, when a man came to him and complained about his calamity. The Imam ﷺ said to him, "You have the option to either take to patience, so you will be rewarded, or you do not, so the decree of Allah, the most Exalted One, the most Great, affects you (while you are held in contempt)."[251]

Jabir [ibn Abdullah al-Ansari], may Allah be pleased with him, has said that the Messenger of Allah ﷺ said once, "Gabriel, peace be with him, has said to me, 'O Muhammed! Live as long as you like, for you shall die. Love whomsoever you wish, for you shall part with him. And do whatever you wish, for you shall meet your deeds.'"[252]

---

[249] *Al-Kāfi*, Vol. 3, pp. 1, 220 with a minor difference in its wording; *Bihar Al-Anwar*, Vol. 82, p. 143.

[250] *Al-Kāfi*, Vol. 3, p. 224; *Bihar Al-Anwar*, Vol. 82, p. 144.

[251] *Al-Kāfi*, Vol. 3, pp. 10, 225 with a minor wording variation; *Bihar Al-Anwar*, Vol. 82, p. 142.

[252] [*Man la Yahduruhu*] *Al-Faqih*, Vol. 1, pp. 298, 1363, taken for granted; *Al-Jami` Al-Saghir*, Vol. 2, pp. 248, 6077; *Bihar Al-Anwar*, Vol. 82, p. 144.

It has been narrated that there was a man among the Children of Israel who was a scholar, an adorer of his Lord, a man of knowledge who reached the degree of *ijtihad* (ability to extract law), and he had a wife of whom he was very fond. She died, so he grieved for her immensely, so much so that he took to seclusion at his house without leaving it, closing his door to the public and staying away from them; nobody could enter. A woman from among the Children of Israel heard about what had happened to him, so she came and said that she needed to hear his judgment about a matter wherein direct communication is required. People went away as she remained at the door. He was told about her, so he permitted her to enter. She said, "Shall I ask you to issue a verdict about an issue?" He said, "What is it?" She said, "I borrowed some pieces of jewelry from one of my neighbors and kept wearing them for quite some time, then the owners sent me a message asking for them back. Should I give them back?" He said, "Yes." She said, "But the jewelry has been with me for such a long period of time." He said, "This is another reason why you should return it." It is then that she said to him, "May Allah have mercy on you! Do you feel sorrowful about what Allah, the most Exalted One, the most Great, had lent you then took it away from you, while He has more right to it than yourself?!" It was then that he saw the wisdom in what she said, and Allah made him benefit by it.[253]

Abu al-Dardaa' is quoted as having said that Prophet Sulayman (Solomon) son of Dawud (David), peace be with them both, had a son whom he used to love very much and who died, so he grieved immensely for him. Allah Almighty sent him two angels in human form. He asked them, "Who are you?" "Two opponents." He said, "Sit as opponents

---

[253] Malik, *Al-Muwatta'*, Vol. 1, p. 237 with minor wording variation; *Bihar Al-Anwar*, Vol. 82, p. 154.

sit." One of them said, "I planted something, then this person came and ruined it." Sulayman ﷺ asked the other man, "What is this man talking about?" He said, "May Allah reform you; he planted it in the road; I passed by it and looked right and left and saw nothing but plants. I took the side of the road, and this was the reason it was ruined." Sulayman ﷺ asked the other man, "What made you plant something in people's way? Did you not know that the way is a passage for people and people have to pass?" One of those two angels said to him, "Did you, O Sulayman, not know that death is people's passage, and they have to go on their way?" It was as though the veil was removed for Sulayman ﷺ; therefore, he no longer grieved for his son. This has been narrated by Ibn Abu al-Dunya.[254]

It has also been reported that a judge from among the Children of Israel lost a son, so he grieved for him a great deal and went out aimlessly. Two men intercepted his way and asked him to judge in their dispute. He said to them, "It is from this that I fled away!" One of them said, "This man brought his flock and passed over my plants, ruining them completely." The other said, "This man planted between the mountain and the river, and there was no other path besides it." The judge said, "When you planted between the mountain and the river, did you not know that it is people's passage?" The man said to him, "What about yourself? When a son was born to you, did you not know that he will [eventually] die? Go back to your seat of judging between people." They ascended their way; they both were angels.[255]

---

[254] Al-Majlisi, in his *Bihar Al-Anwar*, records the same incident on p. 154, Vol. 82.

[255] Al-Majlisi, *Bihar Al-Anwar*, Vol. 82, p. 155.

It has also been narrated that there was a couple, both handicapped, in Mecca who had a young son. In the morning, their son would carry them to the Mosque, spending his day looking after them. In the evening, he would carry them back home. Once, the Prophet ﷺ missed seeing them, so he asked about them. He was told that their son had died. The Messenger of Allah ﷺ said, "Had anyone been left for anyone, the son of those two handicapped persons would have been left for them."[256]

The above has been narrated by al-Tabrani.

It is narrated that the son of Abu al-Dunya has said [quoting the Prophet ﷺ commenting about the above incident], "Had anything been left because it is needed or to avoid want, that youth would have been left for his parents."

It has been reported about some ascetic woman that she said, "Whenever a calamity is mentioned to me, I remember the Fire [of hell]; so it becomes smaller in my eyes than the particles of dust."

---

[256] This incident is recorded by al-Majlisi in Vol. 2, p. 155 of his *Bihar Al-Anwar*, and it has been narrated by al-Bayhaqi in his *Sunan*, Vol. 4, p. 66 but worded differently.

5 – On Mourning

Mourning over calamities

One who is afflicted by a calamity should remember that calamities, trials, and tribulations are all sent by Allah to those about whom He cares, those whom He likes and towards whom He directs His attention. Before one confirms this reality by looking into the Qur'ān and Sunnah, he must observe those who are afflicted in this temporal abode: He will then find out that the most afflicted of all people are those of goodness and righteousness after the prophets and messengers of Allah. Sacred Qur'ānic verses inform you of the same:

Allah Almighty has said,

وَلَوْلَا أَنْ يَكُونَ النَّاسُ أُمَّةً وَاحِدَةً لَجَعَلْنَا لِمَنْ يَكْفُرُ بِالرَّحْمَنِ لِبُيُوتِهِمْ سُقُفًا مِنْ فِضَّةٍ وَمَعَارِجَ عَلَيْهَا يَظْهَرُونَ

"And were it not that (all) men might become of one (evil) way of life, We would provide, for everyone who blasphemes against (Allah), Most Gracious, silver roofs for their houses and (silver) stairways on which they ascend" (Qur'ān, 43:33);

وَلَا يَحْسَبَنَّ الَّذِينَ كَفَرُوا أَنَّمَا نُمْلِي لَهُمْ خَيْرٌ لِأَنْفُسِهِمْ ۚ إِنَّمَا نُمْلِي لَهُمْ لِيَزْدَادُوا إِثْمًا ۚ وَلَهُمْ عَذَابٌ مُهِينٌ

" Do not let the unbelievers think that Our respite to them is good for them: We grant them respite so they may grow in their iniquity, but they will have a shameful punishment" (Qur'ān, 3:178);

وَإِذَا تُتْلَىٰ عَلَيْهِمْ آيَاتُنَا بَيِّنَاتٍ قَالَ الَّذِينَ كَفَرُوا لِلَّذِينَ آمَنُوا أَيُّ الْفَرِيقَيْنِ خَيْرٌ مَقَامًا وَأَحْسَنُ نَدِيًّا ۞ وَكَمْ أَهْلَكْنَا قَبْلَهُمْ مِنْ قَرْنٍ هُمْ أَحْسَنُ أَثَاثًا وَرِئْيًا ۞ قُلْ مَنْ كَانَ فِي الضَّلَالَةِ حَتَّىٰ إِذَا رَأَوْا مَا يُوعَدُونَ إِمَّا الْعَذَابَ وَإِمَّا السَّاعَةَ فَسَيَعْلَمُونَ مَنْ هُوَ شَرٌّ مَكَانًا وَأَضْعَفُ جُنْدًا فَلْيَمْدُدْ لَهُ الرَّحْمَٰنُ مَدًّا

"When Our clear Signs are recited to them, the unbelievers say to those who believe, 'Which of the two sides is best in position? Which makes the best show in council?' But how many (countless) generations before them have We destroyed who were even better in equipment and in glitter to the eye? Say: "If any men go astray, (Allah) Most Gracious extends (the rope) to them, until, when they see God's warning (being fulfilled, either in punishment or in (the approach of) the Hour, they will at length realize who is in the worst position, and (who is the) weakest in strength! And Allah advances in guidance those who seek guidance, and the things that endure, the good deeds, are best as rewards in your Lord's sight and best in respect of (their) eventual returns." (Qur'ān, 19:73-75).

Abdul-Rahman son of al-Hajjaj has narrated saying that affliction was mentioned to Imam Abu Abdullah [al-Sādiq], peace be with him, and what Allah, the most Exalted One, the most Great, has in store for a believer, so he said that people once asked the Prophet ﷺ about who in the life of this world is the most afflicted, tried and tested. The Prophet ﷺ said, "They are the prophets then people whose conduct is the very best. A believer is tested according to the measure of his *iman* (conviction) and good deeds. One whose conviction is sound, and action is good will have intensified afflictions, whereas one whose conviction is weak and so is his knowledge, his affliction will be little."[257]

---

[257] *Al-Kāfi*, Vol. 2, pp. 2, 196.

Zayd, the oil seller, has quoted Imam Abu Abdullah Husayn ؑ as saying, "Great rewards follow great calamities. Whenever Allah, the most Exalted One, the most Great, loves some people, He tries and tests them."[258]

Abu Busayr quotes Imam Abu Abdullah Husayn, peace be with him, as saying, "There are on earth elite worshippers of Allah; whenever something precious descends from the heavens to earth, Allah diverts it from them to others; and whenever a calamity descends, He sends it their way."[259]

Al-Husain ibn Alwan quotes the Imam Husayn ؑ, too, as saying, "If Allah Almighty loves one of His servants, he pours calamities on him, drowning him in them; I and you welcome the morning then the evening in such condition."[260]

Imam Abu Ja`far al-Baqir, peace be with him, has said, "Whenever Allah, the most Blessed, the most Exalted One, loves a servant, he immerses him in affliction. When he calls on Him, He would say, 'Here I am, O My servant! If you wish I speed up fulfilling your desire, I can do it; but if I treasure it [for you], it is better for you."[261]

Abu Abdullah, peace be with him, has said that the Messenger of Allah ﷺ said, "A great tribulation is rewarded with a great reward. If Allah loves one of His servants, He tests him with a great calamity. Whoever

---

[258] *Ibid.*, Vol. 2, pp. 3, 196.

[259] *Ibid.*, Vol. 2, pp. 5, 196; *Tanbih Al-Khawatir*, Vol. 2, p. 204; with some variation in *Al-Tamhis*, pp. 26, 35.

[260] *Ibid.*, Vol. 2, pp. 6, 197.

[261] *Ibid.*, Vol. 2, pp. 7, 197; *Al-Tamhis*, pp. 25, 34 with minor wording variation.

accepts it will have won the pleasure of Allah, and whoever is angered by the calamity will earn Allah's wrath."²⁶²

Imam Abu Ja`far, peace be with him, has said, "Allah tries the believer in this life according to [the degree of conviction in] his faith."²⁶³

Najiyah has said, "I said to Abu Ja`far, peace be with him, 'Al-Mughirah says that Allah does not afflict a believer with leprosy or leukemia or… anything else.' He said, 'He is unaware of the believer in al-Yasin who is referred to in Surat yā-Sīn (Chapter 36 of the Holy Qur'ān); his fingers were dried; then they were healed. He warned the disbelievers and returned to them the next day, but they killed him… A believer is afflicted with every calamity, and he dies in every way, but he does not kill himself."²⁶⁴

Abdullah ibn Ya`fur has said, "I complained to Abu Abdullah Husayn, peace be with him, about the pain from which I was suffering—and I was quite often sick—so he said to me, 'O father of Abdullah! Had a believer come to know what rewards he earns during times of calamities; he would have wished to be cut to pieces with scissors.'"²⁶⁵

---

²⁶² *Al-Kāfi*, Vol. 2, pp. 8, 197. It is also narrated on pp. 20, 33 of *Al-Tamhis* by [Imam] Abu Abdullah [al-Sadiq].
²⁶³ *Al-Kāfi*, Vol. 2, pp. 9, 197; *Mishkat Al-Anwar*, p. 298.
²⁶⁴ *Al-Kāfi*, Vol. 2, pp. 12, 197; *Tanbih Al-Khawatir*, Vol. 2, p. 204 with a minor wording difference between both texts.
²⁶⁵ *Al-Kāfi*, Vol. 2, pp. 15, 198; *Tanbih Al-Khawatir*, Vol. 2, p. 204. It is also narrated with a minor wording difference in *Al-Mu'min*, pp. 3, 15 and in *Al-Tamhis*, pp. 13, 32.

5 – On Mourning

Abu Abdullah (Imam Ja`far al-Sādiq ﷺ) has said, "People of righteousness will always remain in a hardship; but it is for a short period and will lead to a very, very long period of felicity."²⁶⁶

Hamdan quotes Abu Ja`far (Imam Muhammed al-Baqir father of Imam Ja`far al-Sādiq ﷺ) saying, "Allah, the most Exalted One, the most Great, tries to get closer to a believer through affliction like a man trying to get closer to his wife by giving her a present; He protects him in the life of this world like a doctor protecting his patient."²⁶⁷

Abu Abdullah ﷺ has said that the Prophet ﷺ was invited once to a meal. When he entered the host's house, he saw that a hen had laid an egg on a fencing wall. The egg fell on a wedge in the wall and stayed on it without falling and breaking. The Prophet ﷺ was surprised, so the man said to him, "Are you surprised about this egg (which did not break)? By the One Who sent you with the truth, I have never been afflicted with a loss [as small as losing an egg]," whereupon the Messenger of Allah ﷺ stood up and did not partake of that man's food at all. He ﷺ said, "Allah has nothing to do with one who never suffers a loss."²⁶⁸

Reports similar to these are numerous, so let us be satisfied with this much.

---

²⁶⁶ *Al-Kāfi*, Vol. 2, pp. 16, 198.
²⁶⁷ *Al-Kāfi*, Vol. 2, pp. 17, 198; *Tanbih Al-Khawatir*, Vol. 2, p. 204. It is also narrated with a wording difference on pp. 50, 91 in *Al-Tamhis*.
²⁶⁸ *Al-Kāfi*, Vol. 2, pp. 20, 198.

Soothing the Heart of the Bereaved

6 – Conclusion

We would like to conclude this dissertation with a sacred letter written by our master, Imam al-Sādiq, Abu Abdullah Ja`far son of Muhammed ﷺ, to a group from among his cousins when they were afflicted with hardship by some of their enemies by way of consoling them. We narrate it through *isnad* to Sheikh Abu Ja`far al-Tusi—may Allah sanctify his soul—who quotes Sheikh al-Mufid Muhammed ibn al-Nu'man and al-Hussain ibn Ubaydullah al-Ghada'iri citing al-Sadūq Abu Ja`far Muhammed ibn Ali ibn Babawayh from Muhammed ibn al-Hasan ibn al-Walid from Muhammed ibn al-Hasan al-Saffar from Muhammed ibn al-Hussain ibn Abu al-Khattab from the great trusted authority Muhammed ibn Abu Omayr from Ishaq ibn Ammar saying that Abu Abdullah Ja`far ibn Muhammed, peace be with them both, wrote Abdullah ibn al-Hasan, when he and his family were taken captives, consoling him for what had befallen him saying the following:

In the Name of Allah, the most Gracious, the most Merciful

To the righteous descendants and good progeny from the son of his brother and cousin:

If you have been singled out—you and your family who were taken away [captive] with you—with regard to what has happened to you, you are not alone with regard to sadness, anger, depression and heart ache besides myself. I have had my share of feeling alarmed, upset, and burnt by calamity as much as you have. But I remembered how Allah, the most Exalted One, the most Great, has commanded the righteous to be patient and to take to solace when He addresses His Prophet, peace and blessings be with him and his progeny, "**Now wait for your Lord's command with patience, for truly you are in Our eyes**" (Qur'ān, 52:48); "**So wait patiently for your Lord's command, and do not be like the companion of the whale (prophet Younus, Jonah)**" (Qur'ān, 68:48); and remember when He told His Prophet ﷺ when Hamzah's corpse was mutilated: "**And if you retaliate, do it in no worse a way than they did to you: But if you show patience, that is indeed the best (course) for those who are patient**" (Qur'ān, 16:126) and also when He says, "**Enjoin prayer on your people, and be persevere. We do not ask you to provide sustenance: We provide it for you. But the (fruit of) the hereafter is for righteousness**" (Qur'ān, 20:132). Other such verses are: "**[Those] who say, when afflicted with calamity, "To Allah do we belong, and to Him do we return." They are the ones on whom God's blessings and mercy (descend), and they are the ones who receive guidance**" (Qur'ān, 2:156-57); "**Those who patiently persevere will indeed receive a reward without measure!**" (Qur'ān, 39:10); "**… bear with patient constancy whatever betides you, for this is firmness (of purpose) in (the conduct of) affairs**" (Qur'ān, 31:17); "**Moses said to his people, "Pray for help from Allah, and (wait) in patience and constancy, for the earth is God's to grant as a heritage to such of His servants as He pleases, and the end is (best) for the righteous**" (Qur'ān, 7:128); "**… those who have faith and do righteous deeds and (join together) in the mutual teaching of truth, and of patience and constancy…**" (Qur'ān, 103:3); "**We shall test you with something of fear and hunger, some loss in goods or lives or the fruits (of your toil), but give glad tidings to those who patiently persevere" (Qur'ān, 2:155); "... men and women who are patient..." (Qur'ān, 33:35); "... be patient and constant, till Allah decides, for He is the best to decide" (Qur'ān, 10:109).

"Be informed, uncle and cousin, that Allah, the most Exalted One, the most Great, does not mind a loyal servant of His suffers for some time, and there is nothing dearer to Him than one who perseveres while being harmed, exhausted and fatigued. And He, Blessed and Exalted is He, did not care for any period of time about the riches of this life going to His enemy. Had it not been so, His foes would not have killed His loyal servants, intimidated them, jailed them, while His enemies are secure, living in comfort, high in places, having power over others. Had it not been so, both Zakariyya (Zacharius) and his son Yahya (John the Baptist) would not have been killed wrongfully and aggressively due to the oppression of an oppressor. Had it not been so, your grandfather, Ali ibn Abu Talib, peace be with him, would not have been killed when he undertook to follow the commandments of Allah, the most Great, the most Sublime, nor your uncle al-Husayn son of Fatima, peace be with them both, due to persecution and enmity.

"Had it not been so, Allah, the most Exalted One, the most Great, would not have stated in His Book the following: "And were it not that (all) men might become of one (evil) way of life, We would provide, for everyone who blasphemes against (Allah), the Most Gracious, silver roofs for their houses and (silver) stairways on which they ascend" (Qur'ān, 43:33); "Do they think that, because We have granted them abundance of wealth and sons, We would hasten them on in every good? Nay! They (simply) do not understand" (Qur'ān, 23:55-56)."

"Had it not been so, this tradition would not have come to be: "Had the believer not felt saddened by it, I would have made for the unbeliever a headband of iron, so no headache can ever reach him."

"Had it not been so, this tradition would not have been narrated: "Life in this world is not worth to Allah, the most Exalted One, the most Great, the wing of a mosquito."

"Had it not been so, Allah would not have let an apostate take of its water a handful to drink.

"Had it not been so, this tradition would not have been narrated: "Had a believer been on the summit of a mountain, Allah would have sent him an unbeliever or a hypocrite to harm him."

"Had it not been so, this tradition would not have been narrated: "If Allah loves some people, or a servant, He would pour affliction on them/him, so they/he do(es) not get out of grief except to fall into another."

"Had it not been so, this tradition would not have been reported: "There are no dosages dearer to Allah Almighty, which His believing servant swallows in the life of this world, than one of suppressing anger and outrage, and one of grief at the time of a calamity about which he is patient with good consolation and hope for His rewards."

"Had it not been so, the companions of the Messenger of Allah ﷺ would not have prayed for those who oppressed them to have a long lifespan, physical health and an abundance of wealth and children.

"Had it not been so, we would not have come to know that whenever the Messenger of Allah (ص) singled out a man to pray for mercy and forgiveness for him, the man would be martyred.

"So, O uncle, cousin, cousins, and brothers, take to patience, accept, surrender, and commit yourselves to Allah, the most Exalted One, the most Great; accept and be patient about His decree; uphold obedience to Him and obey His command.

"May the Almighty pour on us and on yourselves patience, and may He conclude for us and for yourselves with happiness. May He save us and yourselves from every perdition by His Might; surely He hears, and He is near. Allah blesses the Chosen One from among His creation, Muhammed the Prophet and his progeny, peace and blessings of Allah be with them all."[269]

This is the end of the consolation verbatim as copied from the book titled *Al-Tatimmaat wal Muhimmaat*, and with it do we conclude this dissertation, praising Allah Almighty for what He has enabled us to achieve, blessing the Man of the Message ﷺ and his progeny, the people of infallibility and equity. It was completed by its author, the one who is in need for Allah Almighty, Zain ad-Din Ali ibn Ahmed al-Shami al-Amili, may Allah deal with him through His favor and forgive him through His boon. It was completed during the daytime of Friday, the first of the anticipated sacred month of Rajab in the year 954 A.H., praising, blessing, greeting, and seeking Allah's forgiveness. All praise belongs only to Allah; His peace and blessing be with our master Muhammed, his progeny, and companions.

---

[269] *Iqbal Al-A'mal*, p. 578 with minor wording difference. It is also cited in *Bihar Al-Anwar*, Vol. 82, p. 145 from *Musakkin Al-Fuad*.

Soothing the Heart of the Bereaved

www.ingramcontent.com/pod-product-compliance
Lightning Source LLC
Chambersburg PA
CBHW021437080526
44588CB00009B/564